THE AMERICA'S CUP

BEKEN OF COWES

THE AMERICA'S CUP

1851 TO THE PRESENT

WITH AN INTRODUCTION BY
OLIN STEPHENS

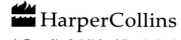 HarperCollins

A Cornelia & Michael Bessie Book
An Imprint of HarperCollinsPublishers

THE AMERICA'S CUP.

Copyright © Beken of Cowes Ltd 1990. All rights reserved.
No part of this book may be used or reproduced in any manner
whatsoever without written permission except in the case of
brief quotations embodied in critical articles and reviews. For
information address HarperCollins Publishers, 10 East 53rd
Street, New York, NY 10022.

FIRST EDITION

Designed by Ron Clark

LIBRARY OF CONGRESS CATALOG CARD NUMBER 89–46517

ISBN 0-06-039117-0

Printed and bound in Italy

90 91 92 93 94 10 9 8 7 6 5 4 3 2 1

CONTENTS

INTRODUCTION

by Olin Stephens

THE HISTORY OF THE AMERICA'S CUP HAS OFTEN BEEN TOLD AND IS known to many, mostly to sailors perhaps, but also to others who know of no other sailing competition. Its frequent controversies, its international character and the fact that it was held for so long by the New York Yacht Club has ensured a world-wide audience.

By frequent repetition, often from a subjective angle, facts must have been lost and objectivity with them; so I think it will be useful to see primary evidence in the form of the photographs in this book, photographs that not only capture reality but also the beauty of the boats that have contested the America's Cup from 1851 to 1987.

This introduction runs over the story once again to provide an armature of support for the pictures and some not too technical thoughts on the boats themselves.

To start we look at the *America*. She was built for racing in New York by a syndicate of six New York Yacht Club members in the ship-yard of William H. Brown. Launched in May 1851, she was finally delivered on 18 June. Three days later she sailed for Le Havre reaching the French port in twenty days. There the *America* was prepared for racing and she sailed for Cowes on the last day of July.

America was the work of George Steers, a young designer employed by Brown. Steers' fast pilot schooner, *Mary Taylor*, had been built with much finer forebody lines than were conventional. *America* was similarly unconventional and though her afterbody water lines were rather full her buttock lines were straight enough to give her a clean run. Her sections seem unusual for her time, a marriage between the flat skimming-dish character of most early American yachts and the plank-on-edge shape favoured by the Thames tonnage rule and used generally in England. Photographs of *America* suggest that her sails were rather flat compared with those of her rivals.

The owners hoped to demonstrate American ability on the water and simultaneously to recover their investment by betting on races they would arrange. The difficulty they met in finding challenges – probably the result of too easy a victory in the Solent – and her eventual win for the Royal Yacht Squadron's Hundred Guinea Cup have been described many times. Two important facts seem more interesting than breaking a jib boom or missing a mark of the course. First, *America*'s design produced a fast yacht. Secondly, appreciation of her fine bow was so great that soon most new yachts incorporated this feature and many older ones were converted.

America's Cup competition was formalized in 1857 when George L. Schuyler and the surviving members of the original six man group, presented to the New York Yacht Club the cup they had won six years before for "friendly competition between foreign countries". Partly because of the American Civil War, however, it was another eleven years before a challenge was received. It came from James Ashbury, the owner of the English schooner, *Cambria*. Conditions, considered unacceptable to the NYYC (including a transatlantic race), were proposed by Ashbury, delaying the match until the summer of 1870.

The difficulty of reaching agreed terms for this first challenge may be seen as an omen for the frequent problems in arranging and applying conditions for so many of the future matches. In the end *Cambria* reached New York on 26 July 1870 having won a race against the schooner *Dauntless*, owned by James Gordon Bennett, Vice-Commodore of the NYYC. This success did not alleviate the problems with the final arrangements for the cup match and eventually *Cambria* sailed in a single race against eighteen boats of the NYYC fleet, including the nineteen-year-old *America*. The race was won by the smaller schooner *Magic* – *America* came fourth and the challenger tenth. But the seeds of controversy had taken root and soon flourished.

The twenty-six matches for the America's Cup, from 1870 to 1987, can be divided into five groups. The first four matches seem to have been sailed with a varied group of boats in which there was little in common between challenger and defender. In the next three matches the defenders all hailed from Boston and were designed by Edward Burgess. Each was a little longer and faster than its predecessor but retained a distinct family character. All were beamy but the beam to depth ratio was not extreme. All used centreboards and all were rigged as sloops. Their first two opponents were narrow, deep – typical cutters – but the third, the *Scottish Thistle*, designed by G.L. Watson, pointed to the future with a new forebody employing a sharply raking stem to provide some overhang and, below the water, a cutaway forefoot to reduce wetted area. I think it is likely that *Thistle* stimulated the thinking that later led to Herreshoff's successful designs for his five defenders.

The changing character of the yachts resulted not only from design experience but also from changes to the rating rules – rules that determined the time allowances to compensate for the differences in size. The efforts to ensure the best speed for rating ratio was always present in design considerations, if not with the same intensity that we see today.

Although the Hundred Guinea Cup was sailed without time allowance, in 1843 the Royal Yacht Squadron had adopted a time allowance system, devised by a member named Ackers. If Ackers' Scale had been employed for the Hundred Guinea Cup then *Aurora* might have received an allowance of forty-five seconds per ton from scratch or possibly thirty-seven minutes overall (Ackers' Scale, it must be noted, seems to have been the first table of time allowances. These varied according to the size of the yacht and were given for a particular course, though apparently not adjusted according to exact course length).

Ackers' Scale, which exaggerated the effect of the beam in the tonnage formula, led to the construction of heavy, narrow yachts. But this also put British yachts at a disadvantage when another scale was employed. In the United States the NYYC also used a tonnage equation in which length and section area were factors. Though hull measurement was improved, sail area was not deemed important enough to be included in the equation and this led to grossly over-rigged yachts. The design of British challengers of this time show no sign of making the best use of scale strictures, though Michael Ratsey's designs, *Cambria* and *Livonia*, appear to me as interesting exceptions, each with a higher than customary ratio of beam to depth – almost American in type.

Dissatisfaction with the tonnage rule combined with the scientific study of hull resistance by William Froude in the early 1870s brought rule changes, though only slowly. The outstanding British naval architect, Dixon Kemp, recommended using a length and sail area equation: length times sail area divided by 4000 equals sail tons. This was tried by the Seawanhaka Corinthians in 1882 but changed a year later to length plus the square-root of the sail area divided by two equalling a 'rating length'. Then, sometime before 1885, the NYYC modified the equation again to read: length times two plus the square-root of the sail area, divided by three equalled the rating length.

In 1893 the NYYC accepted the Seawanhaka Rule so that it was used to provide time allowances in the Cup match of that year. These rules were improved by the use of both length and sail area, but the omission of displacement still resulted in extremes with boats that were, until 1903, progressively longer over all, lighter and carrying even larger rigs.

These were the features of the first four of the five boats designed by America's greatest designer, Nathanial G. Herreshoff, and built at the Herreshoff yard. They successfully held the cup for the NYYC in the six matches from 1893 to 1920. Although the defenders were clearly faster, in general character and appearance challenger and defender had much in common as the rating rules became more complete and restrictive. Designers were now carefully studying the rules under which they would race.

By 1903 Herreshoff's *Reliance* showed the extremes that could occur for the sake of speed. Early in the previous year the NYYC adopted the Universal Rule as formulated by Herreshoff himself. It had the virtue of including the three principal determinants of speed: length, sail area and displacement. The rating was arrived at by the use of the following equation: length times the square-root of the sail area, divided by one third of the displacement times five. This formula was used until after the Second World War, though it gradually accumulated new limits as time went by. Good boats resulted even if they seem to have been rather heavy and narrow.

In this period we find some of the greatest photographic images. The yachts were not only big but their rigs towered. The gaff rig with its great club topsails has a beauty not found on the more efficient jib-headed yachts. By this time the photographer's faster shutters and plates could record the excitement of these boats in strong winds and the way the water boiled along the lee rail.

Between the two World Wars came the "J" boat period. Three matches were contested, in 1930, 1934 and 1937. W. Starling Burgess, the designer of many winners, son of Edward Burgess, and a pioneer in aviation, designed the first two defenders, and in collaboration with the present writer, the third. The three challengers were designed by Charles Nicholson though rule requirements ensured similar proportions.

From 1958 to 1987 there were ten America's Cup matches all sailed in Twelve Metre sloops built to the International Rule. It is worth noting that the displacement requirements of the Universal and International Rules are almost identical and that the two rules ensured very similar boats.

If the regulations were becoming more clearly defined, what of the America's Cup matches themselves? *America*'s match against the Royal Yacht Squadron in 1851 comes first. Questions still thrive about that race. *America* won and received the Hundred Guinea Trophy, but did she or did she not deserve it? It would seem that she cut the Nab Light Vessel, slightly shortening her course, and that had there been a time allowance *Aurora*, her British rival, would have been an easy winner. But the race was run without any time allowances and although the finish was close, *America* had already established a long enough lead to be certain of victory. Overall I think that *America* showed greater speed than her competitor.

In 1870 it was the British *Cambria* against the NYYC fleet and this time the slightly smaller New York yacht, *Magic,* retained the Cup in a single race. *Magic* was a fairly light schooner of the then typical American type with beamy shoal sections and a centreboard. *Cambria*, also a schooner, was longer and much heavier with a relatively narrow beam. In the race, *Magic* was assisted by a change of wind at the start, led on the beat down the lower bay of New York Harbor and held on through varying conditions on the return leg to win by thirty-nine minutes.

James Ashbury, *Cambria*'s owner, was determined to try again. He built a new boat but also started lengthy negotiations based around two points: first, whether the race could include more than one defender; secondly, how many races should be fought in each America's Cup match. Ashbury, as a member of several clubs, argued that each club deserved a chance. G.L. Schuyler, one of the original syndicate who won the 1851 match, urged the NYYC to accept his definition: a match had to be one against one. The NYYC yielded to Schuyler but reserved the right to select any boat suited to the weather of a particular day. So in October 1871 the NYYC won four races to *Livonia's* one in the best of seven series but used two boats, *Columbia* and *Sappho*, in different races.

In 1876 *Madeleine*, sailing for the NYYC, and the *Countess of Dufferin*, the Canadian challenger, were much more alike than the earlier contestants, as both were centreboard schooners with ninety-five foot waterlines and twenty-four foot beams. *Madeleine* easily won the match and it is interesting that the aged *America*, which sailed in the two races (although starting behind so as not to interfere in the match itself) finished ahead of the Canadian challenger on both occasions.

There was another Canadian challenger in 1881, the *Atalanta*. She represented the Bay of Quinte Yacht Club and was owned principally by her designer, Alexander Cuthbert. As in 1876 the challenge came in the spring, but the six month notice required was waived by the NYYC. Unsurprisingly, *Atalanta* was completed late and on the day the race was set for, 13 October, she was on her way through the Erie Canal. So the match was rescheduled to start on 8 November.

Challenged by a new sloop of smaller dimensions than the previous contestants, the officers of the NYYC ordered their own sloop from A. Cary Smith, whose designs were known for their scientific methods. They also wisely decided to hold selection trials for the defender for the first time. The newly designed *Pocahontas* soon trailed two older sloops, *Mischief* and *Gracie*, with *Mischief*, an earlier Cary Smith design, selected in a controversial decision. In the two cup races *Mischief* beat *Atalanta* by wide margins. It is interesting to note that *Mischief* was owned by an Englishman, Joseph Busk, resident in the USA and of course a member of the NYYC.

Continuing controversy, arising from the difficulty of reaching agreement on the terms of a match and made worse by *Atalanta's* late arrival, led the NYYC to ask Schuyler to write a new deed of gift to clarify the race conditions at the end of 1881. The new deed established that only a single boat on either side could be used in an America's Cup match and that participants must sail to the race course, so the challenger could not therefore be carried by a larger boat.

This new deed was circulated to various foreign yacht clubs. In late 1884, the British designer J. Beavor Webb submitted an interesting challenge for the following year on behalf of two clients, each building large cutters. Webb proposed that if the first of these two were defeated in a best-of-three match in the open sea then a second series would be sailed against the second boat. Surprisingly the NYYC accepted these terms but specified that one of the three races would be held on the inshore club course.

In the event, Sir Richard Sutton's *Genesta* raced first and was beaten by *Puritan* in 1885 and Lieutenant William Henn's *Galatea* raced and lost to *Mayflower* the following year. Other aspects of this match deserve attention. As we have seen, the rules governing time allowance were different on either side of the Atlantic. Far from ignoring this difference, Webb had asked that the average of the two systems should be applied. But Schuyler decided against this innovation. What may have helped Schuyler to reach his decision was the fact that a small British yacht, *Madge*, happened to be doing well in American waters at the time and her success had prompted American designers to adapt. It led to the use of a compromise hull-section, and it was this type, with the centreboard retained, that was used by the Boston designer, Edward Burgess, for his sloop *Puritan*, an easy winner in the defence trials against the NYYC's *Priscilla* and the older *Gracie*.

What was also notable about the 1885 series was the sportsmanship with which the races were contested. In the first race *Puritan* withdrew after fouling *Genesta*, damaging both boats, but Sir Richard refused to sail the course and take the race by default. *Puritan* became the winner in two races. In light conditions the Boston boat was faster, but in the second race and conditions approaching thirty knots, the outcome was far closer – *Genesta*'s performance down wind was superior. Even if *Genesta* failed in her objective, she returned to Britain with several important wins over American yachts and if it hadn't been for the Bostonians and Edward Burgess she may well have carried off the America's Cup.

Goodwill was also a feature of the match between the *Mayflower* and *Galatea* sailed in 1886. *Galatea* was longer than *Genesta* and, hoping for a secure defence, two new American boats were built – *Atlantic* in New York and *Mayflower*, another Burgess design, in Boston. Again the new Boston boat prevailed and she won the two cup races in light weather. General Paine, the owner of the *Mayflower*, had agreed to Lieutenant Henn's request for a match in strong winds, but it was late in the season and the boats were laid up before the winds arrived. In the spring and with a strong breeze, *Galatea* lost to *Mayflower* however. It is pleasant to record that both Lieutenant Henn and Sir Richard made many friends in America.

The success of the compromise type which struck a balance between beam and depth undoubtedly brought better boats to the sport, and *Thistle*, the next challenger, is one of the most significant yachts in the history of boat design. I have already referred to her above and will only repeat that her designer seemed to combine observations based on the new American type with the results of William Froude's studies. To anticipate only a little, I see *Thistle* leading directly to Herreshoff's breakthrough in 1891, *Gloriana*, so fabulously successful because Herreshoff brought his engineering genius to bear upon a novel and lighter rig and hull, and the overall shape of the boat as well.

Thistle represented the Royal Clyde Yacht Club as challenger in 1887. General Paine built the defender, naming her *Volunteer*. She may also have been influenced by Froude, as her wetted area was held down by some rocker and not the straight keel of the previous Burgess designs. Her early season was very successful and the single trial race against the *Mayflower* was a formality. *Thistle*, likewise, had been successful, but her rig appears to have been heavy and she was described as tender. She was no match for *Volunteer* in the two races that decided the match.

James Bell, the Scottish owner of *Thistle*, immediately indicated that he wished to challenge again the following year. At the same time, elements in the NYYC, unhappy with Schuyler's last deed of gift, had asked him to try again and to make it more restrictive. It was under this new deed that the battles of 1987 and after have been fought. In its provision there was an article demanding longer notice of a race date and a requirement that races would be without a time allowance if there was a failure to reach mutually agreed terms. Bell withdrew and the new deed provoked a great deal of criticism from potential challengers.

Eventually the criticism cooled and an acceptable challenge was received from the Royal Yacht Squadron in the name of Lord Dunraven. *Valkyrie II* was a ninety-foot waterline yacht – the NYYC had dropped its demand for more detailed dimensions. The match was set for October 1893, but the NYYC needed a defender. Since the last match Burgess had died and the Herreshoff designs for the forty footers *Gloriana* (1891) and *Wasp* (1892), had both been great successes. Soon four defence candidates had been ordered – two Boston-designed boats and two by Herreshoff.

This time neither of the Boston boats could hold either of the Herreshoff designs; it was close between these two, but *Vigilant*, fitted with a centreboard, beat her keel sister and was chosen to sail against *Valkyrie II*. *Vigilant* won the Cup match in three races – the first two were easy victories; however the third, sailed in a hard breeze, was one of the closest in cup history.

On a windward and leeward course with both boats reefed, *Valkyrie* outsailed *Vigilant* and led by almost two minutes at the weather mark. On the hard run *Valkyrie*'s first spinnaker was torn during the set. She promptly sent up a light second spinnaker which burst almost at once, to be followed by her balloon jib topsail which held.

Aggressive is the word to describe *Vigilant*. She set her spinnaker successfully in stops and went on to set more sail. With one man at her topmast head clearing a fouled halyard and another working in from the end of the boom, she shook out the reef, set her balloon jib topsail and shifted from working to club topsail. This added sail drove her past *Valkyrie* just short of the finish to a win of less than two minutes and a margin of forty seconds on corrected times.

Lord Dunraven challenged again in 1895 when his *Valkyrie III* met *Defender*, a new Herreshoff boat. Both boats had shoaler bodies, longer ends and bigger rigs than their predecessors. They were also much faster. This match was won by *Defender* in three races sadly marred by accusations and counter-accusations. In the first race there was a starting line collision and then accusations by Lord Dunraven of illegal ballast increasing on the American boat.

It was another four years before the next match in which Sir Thomas Lipton made his first of five challenges with *Shamrock I*, a Fife design. He was met by another Herreshoff design. Herreshoff was soon to become known as the Wizard of Bristol (home of his Rhode Island boat yard). This time it was *Columbia* which outsailed the challenger in three easy races.

Lipton made his second challenge in 1901 and went to Watson for *Shamrock II*. A NYYC syndicate ordered a new sloop from Herreshoff. Both *Shamrock I* and *Constitution* showed the effect of the measurement rule, which gave no credit for displacement, in their shallow, long-ended hulls, their deep keels and their big rigs. They were much alike but, since there was effectively a premium on light weight, the challengers were weakened by the necessity for a heavier boat to withstand the Atlantic crossing.

Herreshoff may have tried hard to use this advantage in the *Constitution* as this new yacht was fast in light conditions but lost her mast in the early season and continued to suffer through lesser failures and lack of crew confidence. A second new boat was built in Boston for Thomas Lawson. He was not a member of the NYYC, even though he had been advised to join if he were to represent the club as defender. His *Independence* was an extreme boat prone to serious steering problems. Despite considerable public and press support, Lawson's *Independence* never made it to the trials. Though this made comparisons difficult, it was generally accepted that she was not a serious contender. It was the old *Columbia* who became the defender and sailed to a closely contested win over *Shamrock II*, said to have been due mainly to the skilful work of *Columbia*'s skipper, Charley Barr, a Scot.

If, from match to match, new contenders had become longer in the ends and bigger in their rigs, the new Herreshoff design, *Reliance*, went to the limit. She was ordered by a NYYC syndicate to race against Lipton's third *Shamrock* in 1903. (Consult the dimensions of both these boats which can be found in the commentaries on each in the Description of the photographs. The important point to bear in mind is that the rating difference resulting from these dimensions is very close to four feet. Time allowance still in use converts this difference to just under four seconds per mile. Sail area seems to have been underrated.)

Reliance, under her huge rig and with the masterful handling of Charley Barr, won three races easily, setting records for the thirty mile course.

It was now agreed that a rule change was necessary to encourage a more widely useful yacht even for such intense racing. The NYYC had already adopted Herreshoff's Universal Rule, though this was not immediately to apply to the America's Cup. The old rule met strong opposition, delaying any further challenge. In 1913 Lipton made an unconditional challenge and the club agreed, under the mutual consent provision, to race in 1914 with a seventy-five foot waterline boat measured under the Universal Rule.

Three candidates were built for the coming defence: a new Herreshoff boat called *Resolute* and designs by Gardner (*Vanitie*) and George Owen (*Defiance*). In 1914 *Vanitie* and *Resolute* began a long line of closely contested races, but due to the outbreak of the First World War and with *Shamrock IV* in Bermuda, the cup match was called off to be eventually sailed in 1920.

Shamrock IV was a very fast sailboat. Designed by Charles Nicholson, she accepted a penalty under the new rule due to the fullness of her ends, which gave her a long sail length. She won the first of the best of five series when *Resolute*'s throat halyard parted and took the second in light, flukey weather. Then the weather changed to favour *Resolute* and she took the last three races. It was in this close series that boats were sailed by amateur helmsmen – *Shamrock* by Sir William Burton, *Resolute* by Charles Adams.

For nearly ten years all was quiet. Then Sir Thomas Lipton made his fifth challenge for a match in 1930. This time the NYYC responded with the suggestion that the races be held at the top of one of the larger classes, thus reverting to a proposal of Lipton's prior to the last series. It was agreed to use the "J" Class or seventy-six foot rating.

Shamrock V came from the board and yard of Nicholson and had to face the best of four defence candidates. This turned out to be *Enterprise*, designed by W. Starling Burgess for the Harold Vanderbilt syndicate, winner in closely fought trials against *Weetamoe*. Compared with the last series, the defender won four easy races to take the best-of-seven match. Many observers thought that *Shamrock* had far greater potential than she showed, but in comparison to *Enterprise* her equipment and handling fell short. For the first time the jib-headed rig was used and *Enterprise* stepped an aluminium mast during the trials to gain a late season advantage over *Weetamoe*.

The influence of airplanes on yachts can be seen in the next match as the challenger was Sir Thomas Sopwith. Starling Burgess, who again was the American designer, had been active and successful in the same field. When Sopwith's challenger for 1934 was accepted, the world's economies were in depression. This meant that the Vanderbilt boat, *Rainbow*, was the only new yacht, although *Weetamoe* and the Boston backed *Yankee* had been altered and lengthened because of added ballast. Again, after close trials, the Vanderbilt boat was selected to defend.

There was no easy win this time as Charles Nicholson's *Endeavour* was without doubt the faster yacht. A combination of luck and good handling saved the NYYC representative so that after the loss of the first two races she lucked out of a losing position in the third and went on to win the next three amid protests and counter-protests. A personal note: 1934 was this writer's first exposure to America's Cup racing as he sailed in the *Weetamoe* during the trial races, having been invited on board by her designer, Clinton Crane. Unfortunately the alterations were unsuccessful but the experience was invaluable. Our office had designed a number of winners in the six and eight metre classes and for offshore racing in our sixth year. I had worked closely with Professor Kenneth Davidson in pioneer yacht model testing in which Mr Crane was much interested. I'm sure he wanted to help me get a start in the bigger boats.

When Tom Sopwith challenged once more in 1936 for a match the following year, it was again "Mike" Vanderbilt who was ready to build a new defender. Tight finances kept the project in doubt until a contract was signed by the Bath Iron Works to build a new "J" Class sloop, designed in collaboration by Starling Burgess and my own office, Sparkman & Stephens.

After tank tests, which was Starling's first experience of Davidson's methods, a model which he had drawn was selected for the new boat and work went ahead at Bath. *Ranger* was a fine boat and though Sopwith's *Endeavour II* seemed faster than the wonderful *Endeavour I* it was evident that her loss in 1934 had closed a door.

The defender's summer was not completely free of problems as *Ranger*'s first mast was lost while she was being delivered under tow and all summer her bottom surface kept us worried because of the way the paint peeled off her steel underbody. Frequent haulouts were necessary. In the match, however, *Ranger* won four easy races.

The Second World War eliminated any chance of a fresh challenge and post-war inflation sent boat building costs higher than ever. So when the possibility of a challenge was raised by the Royal Yacht Squadron it was felt that a class much smaller than the "J"s should be used. As the deed of gift required a waterline length of at least sixty-five feet this made it necessary to change the deed. Under the direction of Harry Sears, then Commodore of the NYYC, petitions for the approval of two changes to the deed were granted by the Supreme Court of New York State. These actions reduced the required waterline to forty-four feet and no longer required the challenger to arrive at the race course on her own bottom. These changes made it possible to race in the twelve metre class, as desired by the Squadron, and a match was arranged for the summer of 1958.

Three new boats were built to compete for the right to defend and the elderly *Vim* (Vanderbilt's Sparkman & Stephens' boat of 1939) was reconditioned and brought out with an all-star crew. In the trials *Columbia* (Sparkman & Stephens' design for Sears' NYYC syndicate) barely beat *Vim*. *Weatherly*, designed by Philip Rhodes, offered good competition especially in light weather, while *Easterner*, from Boston, was uneven.

The challenger, *Sceptre*, seemed poorly adapted to the sea conditions off Newport where the races had been sailed since 1930 and she lost four straight races in rather strong winds after a first attempt that was abandoned due to calms.

Another match was sailed in 1962 with a challenger backed by the Australian, Sir Frank Packer. He had bought *Vim* and taken her to Sydney, where she was used as a trial horse for the Alan Payne designed *Gretel*. Payne had used the Stevens towing tank as an aid in his design and *Gretel* was a strong contender.

One new boat built for this series was *Nefertiti*, designed by Ted Hood. *Weatherly*, beautifully sailed by Bus Mosbacher, won the trials and held the cup in a close match: four races to one. *Gretel* and her Australian crew put up a good contest and left a fine impression.

The Royal Yacht Squadron now challenged for a match in 1963. After the close call in 1962 two new American boats were planned, *Constellation* designed by Sparkman & Stephens and *American Eagle*, designed by A. E. Luders Jr. Something in the wind prompted both designers to tuck the rudders further forward than in the older twelves in order to reduce the wetted area. Both new boats outsailed their older sisters. Through the entire first half of the season *Constellation* lost to *American Eagle*, known as the bird. At midseason a change in the crew of *Constellation* put Robert Bavier Jr at the wheel and the present writer's brother, Rod, in the cockpit. The tables were turned on *Eagle* in the final trials and *Constellation* went on to win four easy races against the British *Sovereign*.

In 1967 it was the Australians who challenged. They brought a boat called *Dame Pattie* designed by Warwick Hood. The NYYC had the new *Intrepid*, probably the most advanced of the Sparkman & Stephens twelves. Her design combined a short keel using a flap or trim tab on the tailing edge and a separate rudder at the aft end of the waterline. Although not brand new in other classes, this was a departure among twelves and made *Intrepid* unbeatable. Her season record under Mosbacher, her skipper, showed only two losses, one when her mast failed and one when she sailed to the wrong mark. This included the four races against *Dame Pattie*.

The 1970 series marked a new development in America's Cup arrangements as spreading interest in several countries led the NYYC to propose a selection series among challengers. The Australians were successful against the first French challenger. However the defence went poorly. Two boats were built and *Intrepid* was altered by Britten Chance Jr.

After a good year this writer went too far in attempting a big boat and *Valiant* was a major disappointment. Charles Morgan built, designed and financed his boat, *Heritage*, and she too was disappointing. The modified *Intrepid* held the cup, but only after a close series against *Gretel II*. Intrepid won the first race in a good breeze. The second was abandoned due to fog. *Gretel* finished just one minute ahead in the re-sailed second, but was disqualified for a controversial starting line foul. *Intrepid* took the next three by small margins amid less than cordial relations.

The next series was scheduled for 1973 but postponed to the following year because of the Oil Crisis. A new condition provided for aluminium construction as Lloyds had done the necessary scantling rules. Aluminium became the preferred material taking the place of wood because it promised lighter weight.

Two aluminium hulls were designed for the 1974 series: a Sparkman & Stephens' design named *Courageous* and one by Brit Chance called *Mariner*. *Intrepid* was altered yet again, this time by Sparkman & Stephens, and she gave *Courageous* as close a race in the trials as *Vim* had given *Columbia*. In the last trial *Courageous*, sailed by Ted Hood, beat *Intrepid* in a hard breeze when she must have been helped by her lighter hull.

Alan Bond's *Southern Cross* won the challenger's trials against *France*, owned by Marcel Bich. She performed well but lost to *Courageous* in four races.

For the next series, in 1977, there were three challengers: one from France, one from Sweden, and *Australia* the winner of the trials. Against her in the cup series was *Courageous*, altered slightly by Ted Hood. Sailed by Ted Turner she had beaten Hood's *Independence* and the new Sparkman & Stephens *Enterprise*, in the trials. In the match, *Courageous* won four close races.

The New York Yacht Club won again in 1980, though five races were needed this time. *Freedom*, designed by Sparkman & Stephens and well sailed by Dennis Conner, took the trials over the new *Clipper* and the older *Courageous*.

If things seemed to be going well for the NYYC and the USA, not all those interested in the America's Cup were satisfied. Less and less time and money was being given to research, whether it was model testing or computer studies. Many felt that twelve metre design had reached a plateau. It is a fact that the last three boats from the Sparkman & Stephens office were much alike – the *Courageous*, *Enterprise* and *Freedom*. For the latter there was no new model, although an existing *Courageous* model was run in the tank to check flow lines and this led only to small, if favourable, changes. The conventional wisdom was that the important differences were in the handling and the sails. As a designer, I was upset by shrinking design budgets while those for other areas grew.

If design funds were small, boat funds were big. The Conner group built two boats for the 1980 series and three for 1983. I should have preferred one well studied design. I looked back to earlier days when, for boats like *Constellation* and *Intrepid*, I had run tests on seven or eight different models, some incorporating as many changes again, before finding one that had great promise. These were small, comparatively inexpensive models which had served well until the bad year of 1970. The apparent need to test much larger and more expensive models limited testing as 1983 approached.

The Conner group started to build two new boats. *Spirit of America* from Sparkman & Stephens' designs and *Magic* from Johan Valentijn. They were tested inconclusively in California and then in Newport in 1982, when it was decided to build again. This was scheduled to be a collaborative design, but problems arose that have been discussed elsewhere and the new boat, *Liberty*, was the work of Johan. The Kirsch group built a second new boat from David Pedrick's designs and sailed by Tom Blackhailer, well known for his confidence that he could beat Conner. His group brought out *Courageous*, considering her a trial horse, but entered her in the selection trials when she was sailed by John Kolius. She was successfully altered by Sparkman & Stephens under the direction of Bill Lanan but, while she managed to beat the new *Defender* and gave *Liberty* a scare, in the end it was Conner's boat that won the selection battles.

The largest ever fleet of invading twelves had assembled in 1983. Australians came from three clubs and there were single entries from England, Canada, France and Italy. One of the Australians, *Advance*, Alan Payne's third cup design, was not up to the pace. Alan Bond's Lexcen design for *Australia II* with its much discussed wing keel dominated the trials, winning forty-eight out of fifty-four races, while the English *Victory* was the best of the rest.

Australia's impressive performance was recognized as a very real threat by the Cup Committee of the NYYC early on. Their reaction to question the legality of the wing keel was based on two counts: first, that it infringed the rule on draft; secondly, that it did not represent Australian design. To some both seemed far-fetched but considering their view of their obligations the reaction can be understood. Eventually the objections were dropped.

The cup series could not have been closer. The first race went to *Liberty* when *Australia*'s steering failed in a close manoeuvre. *Liberty* won again in a close second race – *Australia*'s mast head had problems. On the next day *Australia* was far ahead when the time limit was reached. Then it was light again and *Australia II* won the third by over three minutes. Conner's brilliant sailing gave him the fourth completed race, but after that *Australia*'s speed was too much to overcome, and she won the next three races to take the trophy from the Americans for the first time ever.

Freemantle, Western Australia, new home of the America's Cup is very different from Newport, Rhode Island, but both are great places to sail. Winds tend to be light off Newport and the reverse off Freemantle. Differences in the wind and sea meant differences in the boats. And the success of *Australia II* signalled the need for new designs. So it was an interesting fleet that gathered early to attack Alan Bond in his home waters in 1987.

Enthusiasm for this attack brought a large fleet to the port on the Indian Ocean. The size of the fleet and the elaborate scheme of trial scoring make it impossible to describe the preliminaries in detail, yet it should be recorded that there were no less than six representatives from the USA, two each from France and Italy, one from England, Canada, and New Zealand. One of the leaders from the start was *New Zealand*. The defenders built six boats of which two, *Australia IV* and *Kookaburra III*, went into their final trials. An interesting start to the competition was World Championship series held in January 1986 with fourteen yachts racing and won by *New Zealand*.

Logically after the success of the intensive research that had led to the *Australia II* wing keel, a similar approach was adopted by most of the new candidates, but few realized the lengths to which this would extend. Budgets for model testing and computer work by specialist consultants now grew to be almost unlimited. While in some ways the cost/benefit ratio may seem to have been low, it is true that the most successful boats, especially the winner, *Stars and Stripes*, and *America II* were among the biggest spenders.

The long series of trials made *Stars and Stripes* the challenger against *Kookaburra*, the defender. The large group of designers and consultants responsible for her plans had produced a good hull with a keel employing small wings. She was a big twelve metre and it seems to the present writer that it was her power, derived from her size, that took her to the top of the big fleet. She disposed of *Kookaburra* in four close races to take the America's Cup to San Diego.

Sadly the outcome of the 1988 event became a matter for litigation, the Appeal Court finally ruling in favour of Dennis Conner's *Stars & Stripes*. Controversy has long been part of the America's Cup story, but let us close by thinking of the great sailing and the beauty of the many fine yachts that the cup has brought into being and let us be thankful for the talent, active for so long, that has made possible this lasting record of that beauty.

Olin J. Stephens, January 1990

America, 1851

Ione, 1851

Cambria, 1870

24

SANDYHOOK

Columbia, 1871

Countess of Dufferin & Madeleine, 1876

Genesta, 1885

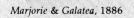

Galatea, 1886

Thistle, 1887

53

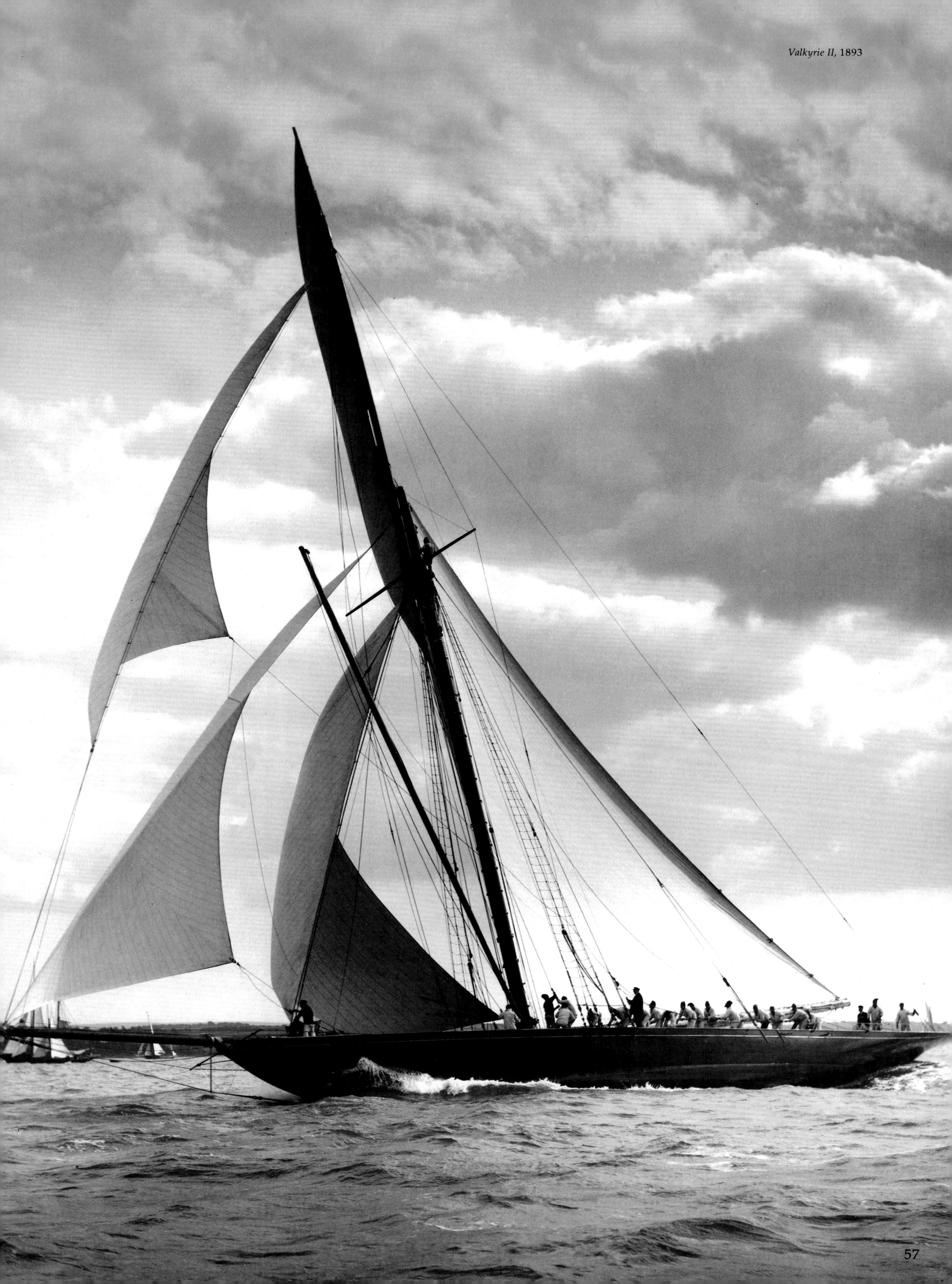

Valkyrie II, 1893

Defender, 1895

Valkyrie III, 1895

Valkyrie III & Defender, 1895

Shamrock I, 1899

Columbia & Shamrock, 1899

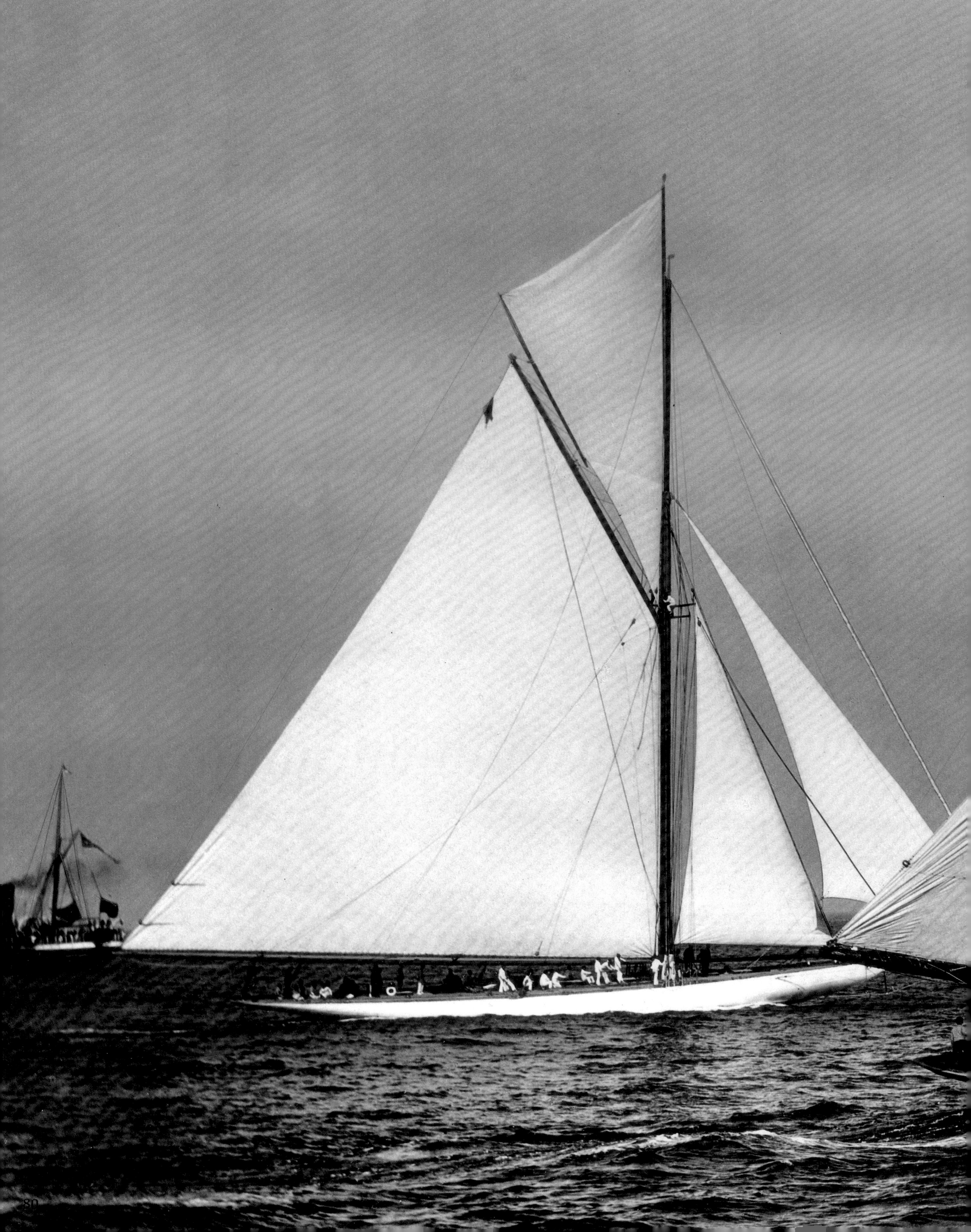

Shamrock I & Columbia, 1899

Columbia, 1901

92

Shamrock IV, 1920

Resolute, 1920

THE "J" CLASS
1930-1937

Shamrock V, 1930

Yankee, 1930

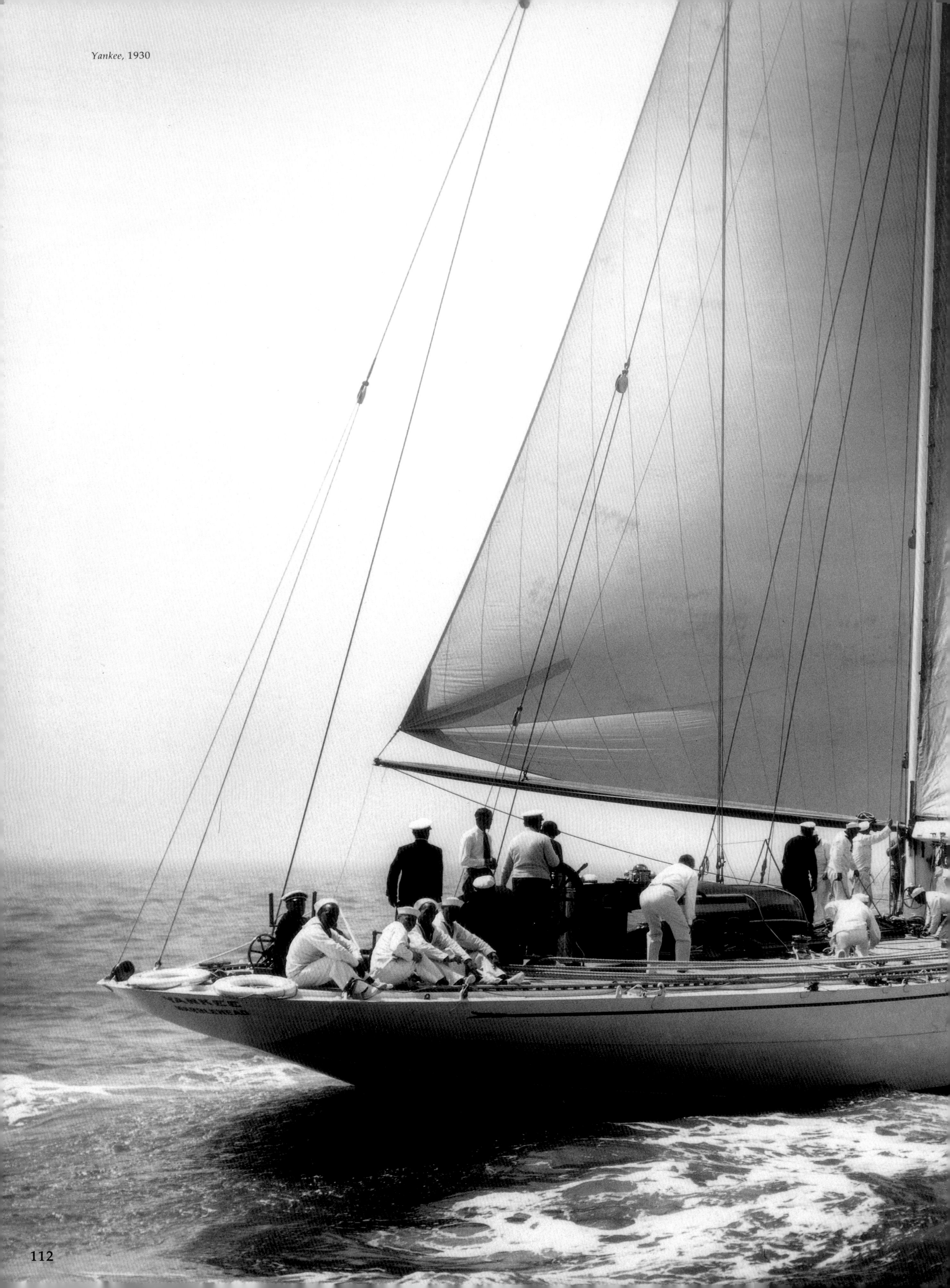

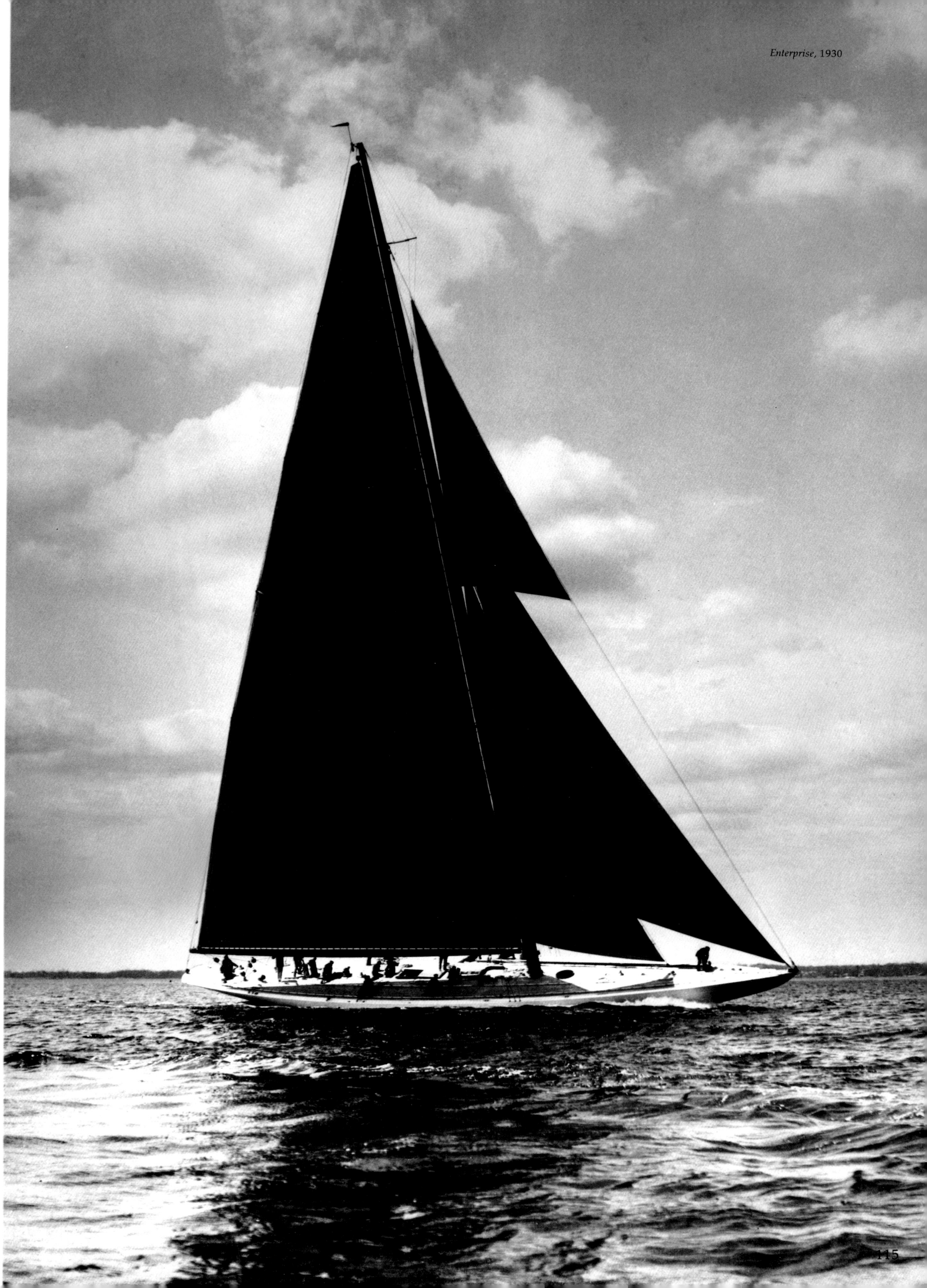

Enterprise, 1930

Velsheda, Candida, Shamrock V, Astra & Britannia, 1934

Yankee, Velsheda & Astra, 1934

Endeavour, 1934

Endeavour II, 1937

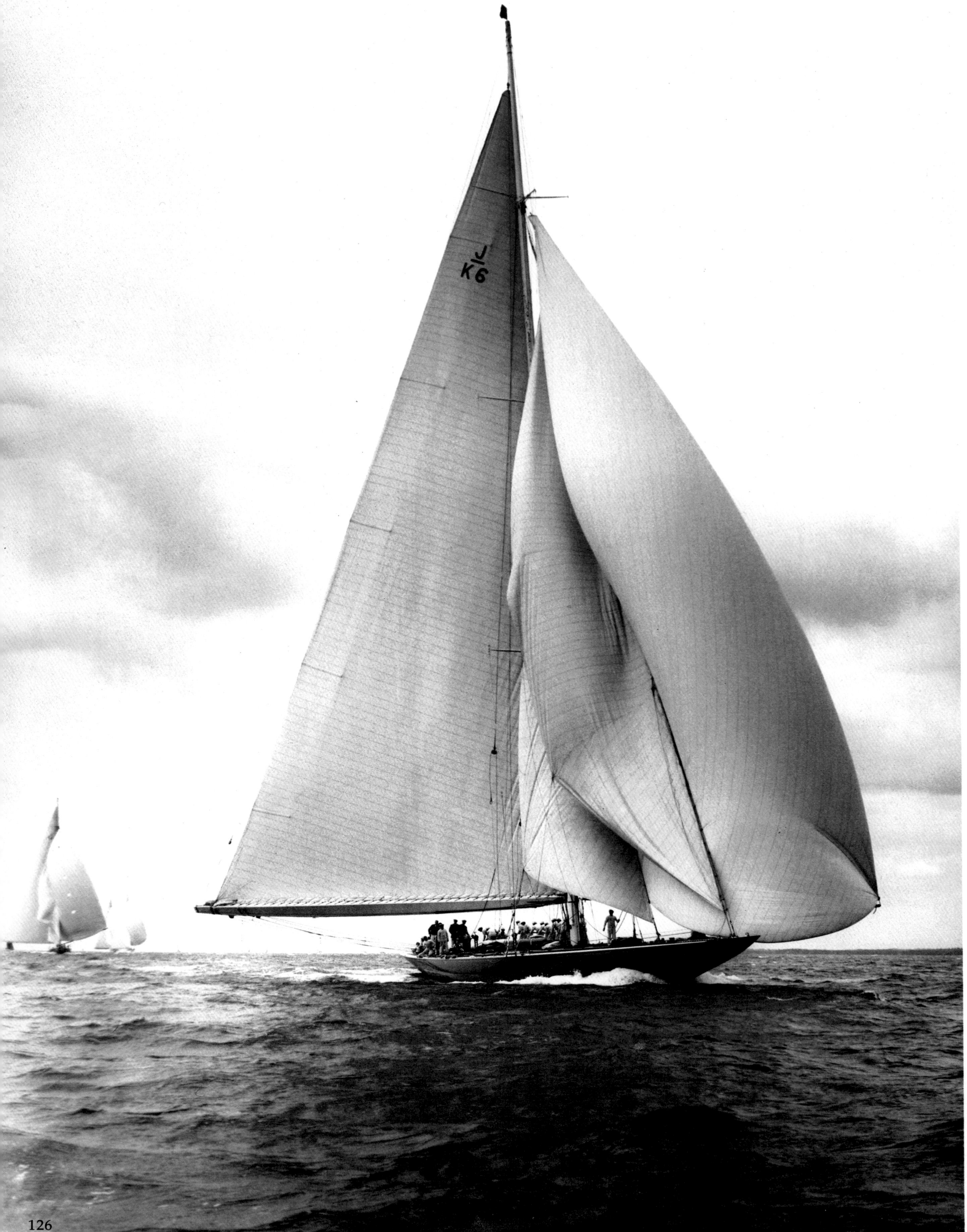

PART THREE
THE TWELVE METRE
CLASS 1958-1987

Flica II, 1958

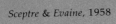
Sceptre & Evaine, 1958

Sovereign, 1964

Intrepid, 1967

Gretel II, 1970

Southern Cross, 1974

Lionheart, 1980

Freedom, 1980

Australia, 1980

153

*stralia II
New
land,
87

ura,
7*

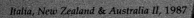
Italia, New Zealand & Australia II, 1987

Azzura II, 1987

DESCRIPTIONS OF THE PHOTOGRAPHS

Long research, coupled with a practical knowledge of racing, enabled us to write the texts to accompany these photographs and record forever these epic and unusual contests.

As for the photographs themselves, it has taken three generations of my family to have made this book possible. Preparing for a large exhibition in Tokyo, I came across some negatives that I had never seen before and some that had hardly seen the light of day. These negatives, taken by my father Frank Beken with a camera of his own design – its legendary shutter release operated by biting a rubber ball held in the mouth – are as good today as they were nearly one hundred years ago. The quality of detail is particularly remarkable.

By the 1930s and the advent of the "J" Class we were still using a similar camera to produce the classical photographs of these great yachts competing for the honour of the America's Cup. Still later, with Kenneth Beken representing the third generation of Bekens to cover the America's Cup, we captured the Twelve Metre contests using the latest Rolleiflex and Hasselblad cameras.

We hope we have succeeded in showing the majesty of this fascinating series of races. It has been a joy so to do.

Keith Beken

New Zealand & Stars & Stripes, 1988

At Ryde pier, the *America* was lying fifth; by the time she reached St Catherine's Point (the half-way mark), she was first; a fast reach to the Needles Lighthouse and she was still in the lead; on the run back to the Solent and stemming the west-going tide, she slowed down, allowing a local boat, the *Aurora*, to catch up a little. When she finally crossed the finishing line, after 10 hours and 37 minutes, *America* was in first place, with her nearest rival, the *Aurora*, close behind.

The Cup was presented to Commodore Stevens of the *America* and has been known as "The America's Cup" ever since.

The strong feature of the *America* was the rake of the masts, typical of the pilot schooners and clippers of her day. The photograph is of the original *America*, taken a year or two after her 1851 victory, with a slightly cut-down rig.

Length Overall	101 feet
Waterline length	89½ feet
Draft	11 feet
Tonnage	c.170 tons
Sail Area	c.5500 square feet
Hull	Wood
Owner	New York Yacht Club Syndicate
Designer	George Steers
Builder	William Brown
Built	New York

Pages 22–23: Schooner *Ione* Great Britain (1851)

Ione was a typical schooner of the 1850s. She was one of the original contestants against the *America* and lay eighth round St Catherines Point, the southernmost tip of the Isle of Wight, with *America* in the lead. *America* then led the fleet to the finish.

Looking at the photograph of *Ione*, we see a classical cruising schooner with a fine bow and comfortable counter. Her sails, for that period, seem to be reasonably well cut, probably by the firm of Ratsey of Cowes.

Length Overall	c.75–80 feet
Tonnage	c.80 tons
Hull	Wood
Owner	A. Hill

Pages 24–25: Schooner *Cambria* UK Challenger (1870)

Cambria was a typical English schooner of the period: deep and narrow gutted, she carried about 9,000 square feet of sail. As this photograph of an oil painting shows, she certainly set all she could on a dead run.

Some formidable contestants awaited her arrival in New York: the schooners *America*, *Magic* and *Dauntless*; and several centreboarders, of which the most notable were *Madeleine* and *Fleur de Lis*. The centreboard keel was becoming increasingly popular in the racing waters off the East Coast of America, where shallow waters allowed the centreboards to be lifted, thus enabling them to reach greater speeds than the deep keel boats.

There was to be a single race (covering a distance of some 35 miles) with *Cambria* sailing against the entire New York Yacht Club fleet. The start was from anchor, as was the rule. The schooner *Magic* took the lead rounding the Sandy Hook lightship, the half-way point, with *America* close behind and *Cambria* in fourth place. *Cambria* finished tenth behind the winner, *Magic*. The first challenge had been lost.

Length Overall	108 feet
Draft	12 feet
Beam	21 feet
Tonnage	189 tons T.M.
Hull	Wood
Owner	James Ashbury
Designer	Michael Ratsey
Builder	Michael Ratsey
Built	Cowes, England
Launched	1868

Page 25: Schooner *Magic* US Defender (1870)

Magic was designed and built as a sloop early in 1857, but later modified to become a schooner. She was small, by some standards, yet very fast. In the first challenge she led the entire fleet, beating the British challenger, *Cambria*, to the finishing line by twenty-seven minutes.

This photograph of a drawing shows *Magic* in the lead, with *America* to her left on port tack and the American schooner *Dauntless* running close behind under spinnaker.

Length Overall	90 feet
Waterline length	80 feet
Draft	6 feet 8½ inches
with centreboard	17 feet
Tonnage	80 tons
Hull	Wood
Owner	F. Osgood
Designer	R. F. Loper
Builder	T. Byerley
Built	Philadelphia USA
Launched	1857

Pages 26–29: Schooner *Livonia* UK Challenger (1871)

Like *Cambria*, *Livonia* was owned by James Ashbury and sailed under the auspices of the Royal Harwich Yacht Club. She was the second challenger for the America's Cup and was built at Ratsey's yard at Cowes. *Livonia* sailed across the Atlantic in exceedingly tempestuous weather, the voyage taking thirty days. Our photographs show her to be a fine sea-going craft, beautifully finished and in top condition.

Frontispiece: The America's Cup

The Hundred Guineas Cup was the trophy for the 1851 race around the Isle of Wight and was made by R. & G. Garrard, the London jewellers. It was some time before the trophy became known as the America's Cup. The owners of *America*, the winning yacht in 1851, took the cup with them on their journey back to the New York Yacht Club, where it was to remain until 1983, the year of the Australian victory.

The cup weighs one hundred and thirty four silver ounces and stands twenty-seven inches high.

(*Photograph T. Jeffrey, Quadrant Picture Library*)

Pages 18–19: The Royal Yacht Squadron

This charming mid-nineteenth century painting shows the Royal Yacht Squadron headquarters at Cowes, Isle of Wight. From these portals came the original Hundred Guineas Cup and many of the challengers over the years. The yacht shown in front of the Royal Yacht Squadron is *Zara*, owned by the then Commodore of the RYS, the second Earl of Wilton.

Pages 20–21: Schooner *America* USA (1851)

The *America* was built in New York in 1851 and sailed almost immediately across the Atlantic to commence racing in Britain, where she was entered for the Royal Yacht Squadron's One Hundred Guineas Cup around the Isle of Wight. The race took place on 23 August 1851; there were seventeen other contestants: English cutters and schooners ranging from 47 to nearly 400 tons. No time allowance was given and the race was started while the yachts were at anchor.

The fleet started to the East with a following wind.

defend each race in the series. *Sappho* won each race by more than twenty minutes.

Length Overall	112 feet
Waterline length	98 feet
Draft	5 feet
with centreboard	22 feet
Tonnage	220 tons
Designer	J. B. Deusen
Builder	J. B. Deusen
Hull	Wood
Sail Area	10,000 square feet

The second challenge was the first to be fought over seven races, each between two yachts. *Livonia* lost her first race, against *Columbia*, by twenty-seven minutes, and the second race by ten minutes, after lodging a protest which was disallowed. She won the third race, mainly due to damage to *Columbia*.

Another American schooner, the *Sappho*, was then chosen to defend the next race instead of *Columbia*, this being allowed in the rules at that time (see Olin Stephens' Introduction), and *Livonia* was beaten by twenty-three minutes. The fifth race, *Sappho* again the defender, saw *Livonia* lose by twenty-five minutes. The cup was held once again by America.

Length Overall	127 feet
Waterline length	107 feet
Draft	13 feet
Tonnage	280 tons
Sail Area	12,000 square feet
Owner	James Ashbury
Designer	Michael Ratsey
Builder	Michael Ratsey
Built	Cowes, England
Hull	American Elm, Oak, Teak

Pages 30–31: **Schooner *Columbia* US Defender (1871)**

Columbia was generally regarded as a light weather boat. With her centreboard up she only drew five feet and was therefore faster than deep keeled boats in light winds.

In these early days of the America's Cup there were selection races in which three or four boats could compete and the defender could be chosen from any of these, even as late as the day before the race. The cup races themselves could only be between two boats. As before, once the gun was fired the yachts were to slip their cables and set sail.

In the first race, held in light winds which favoured the defender, *Columbia* slipped ahead and led *Livonia* all the way to the finish, crossing the line twenty-seven minutes in front.

The second race *Columbia* was behind *Livonia* at the first mark and the British were to protest that the defender rounded it on the wrong side. The protest was overruled. As the wind increased, *Columbia*, with her centreboard up, edged past *Livonia* to finish five minutes ahead.

Livonia won the third race mainly as a result of bad handling aboard *Columbia*: her jib stay parted and her steering gear broke up.

For the fourth and fifth races the Americans turned to *Sappho*, taking advantage of the accepted practice that the same boat need not be used to

Pages 32–33: *Countess of Dufferin* **Canadian Challenger and** *Madeleine* **US Defender (1876)**

The Countess of Dufferin had a fine bow entry and carried 8,000 square feet of sail. She was a centreboarder, designed and built by Alexander Cuthbert in Ontario, Canada, but was generally thought to have been built in a rather rough fashion in comparison to the defender, *Madeleine*. In the picture, *Countess of Dufferin* is seen heading for the Sandy Hook Light vessel, just behind *Madeleine*, who has turned and is running free.

Madeleine had beaten all her contemporaries in the three years of races prior to the America's Cup challenge of 1876. Like the *Countess*, she was a centreboarder and had originally been built as a sloop. In the first race, *Madeleine* revealed her speed on the beat to the first mark and went on to win by twenty minutes. The second race, like the first, began in a fresh breeze, but it turned out to be a long race once the wind dropped. *Madeleine*, who pointed higher than the *Countess*, drew ahead and crossed the line twenty-seven minutes in front of the challenger, thus ensuring that the Cup remained in the hands of the New York Yacht Club. These were the last schooners to contest the America's Cup.

Countess of Dufferin
Length Overall	106 feet
Waterline length	95 feet
Draft	6 feet 6 inches
with centreboard	18 feet
Designer	A. Cuthbert
Builder	A. Cuthbert
Built	Ontario, Canada
Owner	Canadian syndicate (Major Gifford)
Skipper	Alex Cuthbert

Madeleine
Length Overall	106 feet
Waterline length	94 feet
Draft	6 feet
Designer	J. Voorhis
Owner	John S. Dickerson
Built	1873
Skipper	J. Williams

Page 34: *Atalanta* **Canadian Challenger 1881 and** *Mischief* **US Defender**

In 1880 Canada issued a second challenge for the America's Cup with a boat named *Atalanta*. Designed and built by Alexander Cuthbert, she was brought to New York via the Erie Canal, but arrived too late to compete so the series was put back to 1881.

In answer to this challenge the New York Yacht Club returned to David Kirby, the builder of *Madeleine*, who produced a new sloop, *Pocahontas*. Among the trial horses was *Mischief*, who proved so successful in comparison to *Pocahontas* that she was chosen to defend the cup. Built of iron and with a substantial beam of almost twenty feet, *Mischief*, in profile, resembled the English cutter type.

Her owner was an Englishman, Joseph R. Busk, who lived in New York and was a member of the NYYC. In the first of the best of three series there was a fresh breeze and both yachts had lowered topsails. *Mischief* led from the start and finished twenty minutes ahead at the gun. In the second race *Atalanta* and *Mischief* close hauled each other until the first mark, whereupon *Mischief*, heading to the wind, established a clear lead which she went on to convert into a thirty-eight minute victory.

Mischief is in the foreground of the painting, which shows a scene from the first race. *Atalanta* is behind her and both boats have lowered topsails.

Atalanta
Length Overall	70 feet
Waterline length	64 feet
Draft	5 feet 6 inches
with centreboard	16 feet 6 inches
Designer	Alexander Cuthbert

Mischief
Length Overall	67 feet 6 inches
Waterline length	61 feet
Draft	5 feet 6 inches
with centreboard	15 feet 6 inches
Designer	Cary Smith

Pages 35–39: **Cutter *Genesta* UK Challenger (1885)**

At the end of 1884 and after a year of trials, *Genesta*, owned by Sir Richard Sutton, emerged as the next challenger for the America's Cup. A typical cutter with a deep keel and a highly polished copper-sheathed hull below the waterline, *Genesta* is also noteworthy for her long bowsprit, a feature that can be seen in the photographs. In the photograph on page 35, with *Genesta* in dry dock, the depth of her keel is obvious.

The first race of the Cup series was postponed and then cancelled because of fog and light weather. During a luffing match in the second race *Genesta*'s bowsprit pierced the defender's mainsail, but it was judged that *Puritan* was at fault and the race was declared a victory for the challenger. Sir Richard, a noted sportsman, appealed for the race to be re-run, not content with so easy a win.

The series was dogged by unfavourable weather

and when the next race commenced *Puritan* ran out the winner by sixteen minutes. The final race, conducted in fresh winds, produced one of the closest finishes in America's Cup history, with *Puritan* winning by only one minute and thirty seconds.

Length Overall	90 feet
Waterline length	81 feet
Beam	15 feet
Draft	13 feet 6 inches
Tonnage	140 tons
Hull	Composite
Owner	Sir Richard Sutton
Designer	J. Beavor Webb
Builder	D. W. Henderson
Sails	Ratsey & Lapthorn
Built	Glasgow, Scotland

Pages 40–41: Sloop *Priscilla* US Defender Candidate (1885)

Priscilla was built of iron and was an extraordinarily attractive sloop. For all her style, she could not keep up with her rivals in the defence trials for the 1885 cup series and she lost not only to *Puritan*, who went on to defend the cup, but also to *Gracie* and *Bedouin*.

Length Overall	96 feet
Waterline length	85 feet
Draft	
with centreboard	21 feet
Tonnage	115 tons
Hull	Iron
Designer	Cary Smith
Builder	Harlan & Hollingsworth
Built	Wilmington, USA
Launched	1885

Pages 42–43: Sloop *Puritan* US Defender (1885)

Puritan was the winner of the fifth America's Cup challenge. Very straight stemmed with a long overhanging counter and an equally long bowsprit, *Puritan* carried plenty of sail area. Our photograph shows her just after the second and final race of the series, having beaten *Genesta* by the shortest of margins.

Length Overall	94 feet
Waterline length	81 feet
Beam	22 feet
Draft	8 feet
with centreboard	20 feet

Tonnage	108 tons
Sail Area	8,000 square feet
Owner	General Paine and Syndicate
Designer	Edward Burgess
Builder	Lawley & Son
Built	Boston, Mass., USA
Skipper	A. J. Crocker

Pages 44–45: *Mayflower* US Defender (1886)

Built in Boston, Massachusetts, the *Mayflower* was launched in 1886 to compete in the defence trials for that year's America's Cup challenge. Finer in the bow than her contemporaries, *Puritan*, *Priscilla* and *Atlantic*, against whom she fought for selection, *Mayflower* had a vast bowsprit (thirty-six feet) and a substantial keel with extra ballast inside her hull for added stability.

The first race on 9 September 1886 was fought in light conditions which favoured the centreboarded *Mayflower*, who took the race by twelve minutes. Two days later, with a fresh breeze blowing, the second race began from the Sandy Hook Lightship. At the half-way point, *Mayflower* had established a thirteen minute lead over *Galatea*. By the end of the race *Mayflower* had more than doubled her lead. Once again a British challenge had foundered in the waters off New York.

Length Overall	100 feet
Waterline length	85 feet 6 inches
Draft	9 feet 9 inches
with centreboard	20 feet
Tonnage	110 tons
Sail Area	8,600 square feet
Owner	General Paine
Designer	Edward Burgess
Builder	George Lawley
Launched	1886
Skipper	Martin Stone
Hull	Wood with lead keel

Pages 46–51: Cutter *Galatea* UK Challenger (1886)

In the 1885 pre-Cup races *Galatea* competed against several other good British yachts, *Marguerita*, *Marjorie*, *Wendur* and *Lorna*, beating them all and thus becoming the challenger for the 1886 America's Cup.

Her beam was larger than that of the previous challenger, *Genesta*, and the photograph of her interior (48–49) shows she had elegant quarters. It must be remembered that challengers had to sail to the race course, even if this meant crossing the

Atlantic. Mrs Henn, wife of *Galatea*'s owner, was also an enthusiastic sailor and accompanied her husband, along with their two dogs and a monkey named Peggy, on the thirty day voyage to the headquarters of the New York Yacht Club. (The journey out took thirty days while the return only seventeen.)

If there were differences between *Galatea* and other British boats they were little in comparison to those between her and the *Mayflower*. The contrast between the rigging for the top sail can be seen by comparing photographs, and there was also a seven foot difference in beam. In profile, *Galatea* was deep and narrow whereas *Mayflower* was more of a skimming dish.

Length Overall	102 feet 6 inches
Waterline length	87 feet
Draft	13 feet 6 inches
Tonnage	155 tons
Sail Area	7,500 square feet
Hull	Steel
Owner	Lieutenant W. Henn
Designer	Beavor Webb
Sails	Ratsey & Lapthorn
Built	Glasgow, Scotland
Launched	1885
Skipper	D. Bradford
Keel	80 tons of lead enclosed

Pages 52–53: *Thistle* UK Challenger (1887)

Thistle was the third British challenger in three consecutive years and, as Olin Stephens remarks in his introduction, her design was to lead to important breakthroughs in yacht building. Her sharply raking stem and cutaway forefoot were innovatory and she struck a good balance between beam and depth.

Racing against *Genesta* and *Irex* in English waters, *Thistle* proved herself a worthy challenger. She crossed the Atlantic in twenty-two days to compete against the defender, *Volunteer*, in a three race series.

successfully in the USA, *Navahoe* went to Britain and took part in many competitions in the Solent off Cowes. In a famous race from Cowes to the Cherbourg breakwater light house and back, some one hundred and twenty miles, *Britannia* beat *Navahoe* by a single minute.

In this photograph, *Valkyrie* is on the right, charging through *Navahoe*'s lee side. The quality and cut of the canvas sails must be noted: there is not a wrinkle to be seen.

In her first race, watched by a massive fleet of onlookers, *Thistle* beat her opponent to the starting line. *Volunteer* came back, however, tacked across her and won by nineteen minutes. In the second race, run in moderate winds, *Volunteer* led from start to finish. So a challenge that had seemed so promising ended unsuccessfully. *Thistle* was subsequently sold to Kaiser Wilhelm, a keen sailor, who came to Britain to race her.

Length Overall	108 feet 6 inches
Waterline length	86 feet 6 inches
Beam	20 feet
Draft	13 feet 6 inches
Tonnage	130 tons
Sail Area	9,000 square feet
Hull	Steel
Owner	Vice-Commodore James Bell and consortium
Designer	G. L. Watson
Built	Clyde, Scotland
Sails	Ratsey & Lanthorn
Skipper	John Barr
Launched	1887

Pages 54–55: *Volunteer* US Defender (1887)

As the photograph shows, *Volunteer* was a handsome yacht with what one could call a clipper bow and a very long bowsprit – almost thirty-eight feet. Narrower and deeper than *Puritan* and *Mayflower*, whom she raced in the defence trials, *Volunteer* was a fast boat, which she needed to be to fight off *Thistle's* challenge.

It is difficult not to admire the excellent rigging employed in those days. The mast is as straight as an arrow, and there is no sign whatsoever of any sag in the fore and jib stays. As with *Thistle*, *Volunteer's* decks are remarkably clear of any obstructions.

Length Overall	108 feet
Waterline length	86 feet 6 inches
Beam	23 feet 6 inches
Draft	10 feet 6 inches
with centreboard	21 feet
Hull	Steel
Owner	General C. Paine
Designer	Edward Burgess
Builder	Pusey & Jones
Built	Wilmington, USA
Launched	1887
Skipper	Capt. H. Haff

Pages 56–57: *Valkyrie II* UK Challenger (1893)

Valkyrie II, a successor to a previous boat with the same name, was commissioned by the Earl of Dunraven and designed by the now famous G. L. Watson. (Watson had recently been commissioned by George, Prince of Wales, to design *Britannia*, the Royal Yacht, which had much in common with *Valkyrie II* and raced against her a few times in the months leading up to the Cup.)

Since the last challenge there had been changes to the rules under which the America's Cup was to be raced. Dunraven, when lodging his challenge, had suggested that the series should be decided from the best of five races. This the New York Yacht Club agreed to.

When the cup series commenced, *Valkyrie* came to New York short of race practice. The first race was held on 7 October 1893 – two days later than scheduled. At the start, *Valkyrie* established a short lead in the fresh breeze, but she could not hold the defender, *Vigilant*, who was fast on the reach and went on to take the race by five minutes. In the second race *Vigilant* won by over ten minutes. In the third, *Valkyrie*, with her mainsail reefed, her decks awash, and despite bursting two spinnakers, managed to finish only forty seconds behind the defender. A brave race but not enough to win the America's Cup.

The second photograph shows the start of the second race, with both challenger (in the foreground) and defender close hauled.

After the cup race *Valkyrie* returned to Britain. During an epic race on the Clyde the following year, she was rammed and sank soon after.

Length Overall	117 feet
Waterline length	85 feet 6 inches
Beam	22 feet 6 inches
Draft	16 feet 6 inches
Tonnage	140 tons
Sail Area	10,000 square feet
Hull	Wood
Owner	Lord Dunraven
Designer	G. L. Watson
Builder	D & W Henderson
Built	Clyde, Scotland
Launched	April 1893
Skipper	W. Granfield

Pages 58–59: *Navahoe* US trial horse (1893)

Navahoe is of interest because she was designed by the legendary Nathaniel Herreshoff, who went on to design many America's Cup defenders. After racing

Pages 60–63: *Vigilant* US Defender (1893)

Nathaniel Herreshoff arguably invented the modern yacht, and the photograph of *Vigilant* in dry dock shows why. Her long, lean bow and counter, together with her gracious lines, all point towards twentieth century yacht design.

Vigilant was a centreboarder, the board projecting downwards through her lead keel to give her a draft of twenty-four feet. The entire underwater section was covered in "tobin" bronze, giving her a very smooth finish and added speed through the water.

Of course, *Vigilant* did not become defender immediately, and she had to earn her place by fighting off the other trialists, *Colonia*, *Jubilee* and *Pilgrim*. In fact the defender trials were hotly contended that year, but *Vigilant* was finally the unanimous choice to defend the cup against *Valkyrie II*.

The first race went to *Vigilant*, winning by five minutes, while the third was the most dramatic. Rough winds kept the two boats together until the closing minutes, whereupon *Vigilant* crept in front to win by the narrowest of margins.

Length Overall	125 feet
Waterline length	85 feet
Beam	26 feet
Draft	13 feet
with centreboard	24 feet
Tonnage	138 tons
Sail Area	11,300 square feet
Owner	New York Yacht Club Syndicate
Designer	Nat Herreshoff
Builder	Herreshoff Mfg Co
Built	Bristol, Rhode Island, USA
Launched	June 1893
Skipper	Nat Herreshoff
Hull	Bronze underwater with steel topsides

Pages 64–65: The Excursion Fleet (1895)

This picture gives some idea of the tremendous interest shown in the America's Cup races.

In the early days, the fleet was the cause of many controversial remarks by challengers and defenders alike. The steamers bearing down on the racing yachts created much confusion. The race committee later came to realize the hazards, and endeavoured to keep the fleet away from the course for future races.

Pages 66–67: *Defender* US Defender (1895)

Herreshoff's design for the 1895 defence was for a narrower and deeper hulled yacht, but one that was lighter as well. Using manganese bronze for her underwater section and aluminium for her topsides, Herreshoff realized his plans. As the photograph of her launch in 1895 illustrates, she was indeed narrow. Both her bowsprit and boom were long, giving her plenty of sail area.

The trial horse for *Defender* was the victor of the previous cup series, *Vigilant*. Keenly contested races ensued, with the skippers of both yachts sailing aggressively. *Defender* finally established her supremacy and went on to race the British challenger, *Valkyrie III*.

Length Overall	123 feet
Waterline length	89 feet
Draft	19 feet
Tonnage	150 tons
Sail Area	12,500 square feet
Skipper	H. C. Haff
Owner	New York Yacht Club Syndicate (William K. Vanderbilt)
Designer	Nat Herreshoff
Builder	Herreshoff Mfg Co
Built	Bristol, Rhode Island, USA

Pages 68–71: *Valkyrie III* UK Challenger (1895)

Valkyrie III, like her predecessor, was designed by G. L. Watson for the Earl of Dunraven. The new *Valkyrie* was a large, powerful yacht with long overhangs on bow and stern to give her greater directional stability in fresh winds. The underside of the hull was rather flat in comparison to other designs of the time.

In the first photograph, with *Valkyrie* running, it is possible to appreciate the vast sail area she carried, and it must be remembered that the sails of 1895 were not made of the lightweight material used today.

In the first race *Defender* and *Valkyrie* sailed side-by-side until the sea became rough, giving the American boat an advantage. On the home run, *Defender* pulled out a comfortable eight minute lead, and went on to win by the same margin. The second and third races were to lead to one of the controversies that are such a feature of America's Cup racing. In the second, just before the race began, *Valkyrie* had the weather position with *Defender* a little behind her. What appears to have happened next was that *Valkyrie*, so as not to cross the line before the gun was fired, bore to leeward. *Defender* dropped off a little, but when the gun was fired *Valkyrie's* mainsail boom end swung out and caught the topmast stay of *Defender*, which then broke. A protest was raised immediately by *Defender's* skipper, but the race continued with the *Defender's* crew carrying out emergency repairs. *Valkyrie* was to reach the finish line two minutes ahead of her rival, but the end of the race merely marked the beginning of arguments on shore. The committee finally resolved that the accident had been *Valkyrie's* doing and her victory was thus disqualified. This was a bitter defeat for Dunraven. When the third race began, *Valkyrie* came to the start line but immediately after crossing it, hauled down her racing flag, thereby not only curtailing the race but concluding the series.

The second photograph was taken five seconds after the foul at the start of the second race. *Valkyrie* leads and the effect of the broken topmast stay on *Defender* is obvious.

Length Overall	129 feet
Waterline length	87 feet 6 inches
Draft	20 feet
Beam	20 feet
Tonnage	167 tons
Hull	Wood over steel frame
Owner	Earl of Dunraven
Designer	G. L. Watson
Builder	D & W Henderson & Co
Built	Clyde, Scotland
Sail Area	13,000 square feet
Skipper	W. Granfield

Pages 72–75: *Columbia* US Defender (1899)

The details of *Columbia's* beam and the ninety tons of lead at the bottom of her fin keel suggest she must have been a remarkably stable boat despite the 13,000 square feet of sail above. Her mast and boom were made of steel, so her stability was matched by considerable strength.

Defender was *Columbia's* trial horse, but before long Herreshoff's new boat proved just how good she was and was thus chosen to defend the America's

Cup. In this photograph *Columbia* is seen bearing down on *Defender*.

The vast fleet of spectator craft that in the past had followed the yachts around the course were this time held at bay – part of Dunraven's protest in the previous series had been that the flotilla of observation craft had interfered with the start and that it was this, not bad captaincy, that led to the collision. But wherever the spectators watched from, the first race was to prove a disappointment. The wind was flukey and the race was called off. In the second, *Columbia* established an early advantage over the challenger, *Shamrock*, and took the race by ten minutes. Two thirds of the third race had been completed before the winds dropped and the race was abandoned. The fourth was won by *Columbia* after *Shamrock* had led to the first mark.

Length Overall	131 feet
Waterline length	89 feet 6 inches
Draft	19 feet
Beam	24 feet
Tonnage	148 tons
Sail Area	13,000 square feet
Hull	Bronze underwater, steel topsides
Owner	Syndicate (J. P. Morgan & O. Iselin)
Designer	Nat Herreshoff
Builder	Herreshoff Mfg Co
Built	Bristol, Rhode Island, USA
Launched	1899
Skipper	Charles Barr
Keel	Fin with 90 tons lead

Pages 76–83: *Shamrock I* UK Challenger (1899)

Shamrock I had a larger sail area than *Columbia*, although this did not always serve to her advantage. The rigging, unable to stand the strain, was prone to break in strong winds. Built at Millwall on the

narrow fin keel. Moreover, *Shamrock* was a very light yacht making use of immadium – a strong but light alloy.

In the selection trials *Shamrock II* showed she had considerable speed, but there were problems with her one hundred foot mast, which she was to lose on occasion (see photograph on pages 86–87). After crossing the Atlantic under tow she impressed the local yachtsmen with her capabilities and appearance. A closely contested America's Cup was anticipated.

The first race was on 3 October 1901. There was a light breeze and both boats crossed the starting line within a few seconds of each other. *Shamrock II* then took the lead and, round the first mark of a triangular course, found herself forty-five seconds in front. To the large contingent of observers, a *Shamrock II* victory looked certain. Yet by the turn of the second mark, *Columbia* had caught up with the challenger and soon pulled out a lead of her own to take the race by over a minute. *Shamrock II* was equally impressive at the start of the second race as she had been in the first. On the first reach she built up a lead of over ninety seconds, but again *Columbia* came back to win. The third race was the tightest of all, and as the two boats came to the finish they were neck and neck, but *Columbia*, with a forty-one second time allowance, crossed the line two seconds ahead and won overall by forty-three seconds.

In the photograph on pages 88–89, Sir Thomas Lipton stands in the centre wearing a bow-tie. Surrounding him are the crews of *Shamrocks I* and *II*.

Length Overall	137 feet
Waterline length	89 feet
Beam	24 feet
Draft	20 feet
Tonnage	150 tons
Sail Area	14,000 square feet
Owner	Sir Thomas Lipton
Designer	G. L. Watson

Builder	W. Denny Bros.
Built	Dunbarton, Scotland
Launched	1901
Skipper	E. A. Sycamore

Pages 90–92: *Shamrock III* UK Challenger (1903)

For his third challenge Sir Thomas Lipton returned to William Fife, designer of *Shamrock I*. The new boat, *Shamrock III*, was built as a cutter and as the photograph of her launch at Dunbarton shows, she had fine lines. Her hull was made from nickel steel and, for racing, painted white. But where *Shamrock III* differed from her predecessors most obviously was in her steering. While American yachts had used a wheel for some time, *Shamrock* was the first challenger to employ one.

In order that *Shamrock III* might be in the best possible condition for the America's Cup races, Sir Thomas took *Shamrock II* with him across the Atlantic so as to give his new boat the most effective trials he could. She performed well and as the cup series approached Sir Thomas was confident of victory.

The first race was inconclusive: the time limit was reached before either boat came in sight of the finish. In the second, *Shamrock* made early ground over the defender, *Reliance*, but the American boat soon caught up, overtook and went on to win by seven minutes. *Reliance* won the third by just over a minute, and in the fourth crossed the line so far in front of *Shamrock* that the challenger did not even finish. For all the pre-race preparation, Lipton still found himself without the America's Cup on his return journey to Britain.

Length Overall	134 feet 6 inches
Waterline length	90 feet
Beam	25 feet
Draft	20 feet
Tonnage	166 tons
Sail Area	14,200 square feet
Owner	Sir Thomas Lipton
Designer	W. Fife
Builder	W. Denny Bros.
Built	Dunbarton, Scotland
Hull	Steel
Skipper	Robert Wringe

Page 93: *Reliance* US Defender (1903)

Nathaniel Herreshoff and the defence of the America's Cup were now synonymous, and for the 1903 series the legendary yacht designer launched *Reliance*. Like *Shamrock III*, she had a fairly flat-bottomed hull with a low freeboard and a deep fin keel. Her overhangs were enormous: twenty-eight

Thames, *Shamrock I* was designed by the Scot, William Fife, and commissioned by the persistent Sir Thomas Lipton, who was to lead four subsequent challenges.

Shamrock I's flat hull was built of manganese bronze below the waterline and aluminium above, and her keel was a fin type with a large and heavy lead bulb at the bottom.

Shamrock I sailed across the Atlantic in good time under a yawl rig and arrived early for some practice and tuning before the first race.

The photograph on pages 80–81 shows the white-hulled *Columbia* and *Shamrock I* at the start of the second race, while in the picture on pages 82–83, the defender is gradually building up a lead over the challenger.

Length Overall	128 feet
Waterline length	89 feet
Beam	25 feet
Draft	20 feet
Tonnage	157 tons
Sail Area	13,500 square feet
Owner	Sir Thomas Lipton
Designer	William Fife Jr
Builder	J Thornycroft
Built	Millwall, England
Sponsor Club	Royal Ulster Yacht Club
Skipper	Capt. A. Hogarth

Pages 85–89: *Shamrock II* UK Challenger (1901)

Shamrock II found herself racing against *Columbia* (seen in the photograph on page 84), the winner of the previous series two years before, who had proved herself faster than any of the more recently designed yachts. So the backbone of the defence continued to be Herreshoff. Lipton turned to G. L. Watson, the designer of *Valkyrie II* and *III* as well as *Thistle*, for the design of his new boat. *Shamrock II* had a very flat hull, with long overhangs and a deep, feet at the bow, twenty-six feet at the counter. So when *Reliance* heeled in a strong breeze this greatly increased her waterline length and her speed correspondingly.*

Her sail area was vast: 16,160 square feet hung from a single steel mast. The topmast telescoped out from the main mast. As the photograph illustrates, she was a large boat in every respect – note the size of her spinnaker boom.

In the trials she comfortably beat *Constitution* and *Columbia*, and it was in the fourth race of the cup series that speed began to show, pulling out a lead so great that *Shamrock* was forced to retire.

Length Overall	143 feet 6 inches
Waterline length	89 feet 6 inches
Draft	19 feet 6 inches
Beam	25 feet
Hull	Bronze and steel
Keel	Lead bulb
Sail Area	16,160 square feet
Owner	Syndicate (C. Vanderbilt/ O. Iselin/W. Rockefeller)
Designer	Nat Herreshoff
Builder	Herreshoff Mfg Co
Built	Bristol, Rhode Island, USA
Launched	1903
Skipper	Charles Barr

Pages 94–96: *Shamrock IV* UK Challenger (1920)

For his fourth challenger, Sir Thomas Lipton turned to British yacht designer, Charles Nicholson, a partner in the Gosport-based firm Camper & Nicholson. *Shamrock IV* was the result. She was a distinctive boat with a shortened bowsprit and a cut-off stern, which made her mast seem enormous. Painted dark green she looked every inch a racing machine.

Lipton's challenge had been scheduled for the autumn of 1914. *Shamrock*'s progress through the trials was encouraging. She sailed a series of races in which she proved successful. However, *Shamrock IV* got as far as Bermuda when the First World War broke out. She continued her Atlantic crossing and arrived in New York, where it was decided that the race should be postponed until after the war. In 1919, Lipton reinvoked the challenge, which was set for the following July.

The America's Cup began with a win for the challenger. Half way through the race, *Resolute*, the defender, lost her main halyard. She continued, but *Shamrock* passed her and went on to the finishing line unthreatened. *Resolute* hauled down her flag and retired. If the outcome of the first race had given the challenger a rare lead in an America's Cup series, the outcome of the second was even more novel. As the race began both yachts had raised their spinnakers. Between the first and second marks, *Shamrock* carved out a four minute lead from which *Resolute* never recovered. By the finish the lead had been extended to nine minutes. In the five match series, *Shamrock* stood only one race away from the first challenger's victory. But in the third race, while *Shamrock* crossed the line in front of *Resolute*, she lost because of the time allowance given to the defender. The fourth race was a straight-forward win for *Resolute*, finishing ten minutes ahead. Thus the Cup was to be decided in the fifth and final race of the series. While the

* Hers was the first winch to feature in America's Cup competition, and so advanced was its design that the same winch was to be used in the 1920, 1930, 1934 and 1937 America's Cup matches.

early stages were closely fought, *Resolute* took the lead and once in front began to move away. However hard *Shamrock* tried, the distance between the two boats increased. *Resolute* was to win by nineteen minutes and forty-five seconds. A series which had started so well for the challenger was eventually won by the defender.

Length Overall	110 feet 6 inches
Waterline length	75 feet
Beam	22 feet 6 inches
Keel – centreboard	13 feet 6 inches
Tonnage	108 tons
Sail Area	10,500 square feet
Owner	Sir Thomas Lipton
Designer	Charles Nicholson
Builder	Camper & Nicholson
Built	Gosport, Hants., England
Skipper	William Burton
Hull	Wood, three laminations

Page 97: *Lulworth* (formerly *Terpsichore*) UK Trial Horse for *Shamrock IV*

Lulworth, originally named *Terpsichore*, was built in 1920 and is a classic yacht of the era. The cut and set of the sails are perfect – not a wrinkle to be seen – and the shape of the bow and her counter are pretty by any standards.

Lulworth is a classic example of the way design lessons learned in the testing ground of the America's Cup were being applied outside the competition. In the twenties she sailed in many races against *Britannia* and her twenty-three metre contemporaries. As this book goes to press there is good news: *Lulworth* has just been towed from her mud berth at Hamble in the Solent and is to be completely reconstituted at a cost of over three million pounds. Hallelujah!

Length Overall	95 feet 6 inches
Waterline length	85 feet
Draft	13 feet 9 inches
Beam	21 feet 9 inches
Tonnage	186 tons
Owner	R. H. Lee
Designer	H. W. White
Builder	White Bros.
Built	Southampton
Hull	Wood

Pages 98–99: *Britannia* UK Trial Horse

His Majesty's Yacht *Britannia* played an important part in preparing challengers for the America's Cup.

She was used as a trial horse for the *Shamrock*s and later, after conversion, for most of the "J" Class yachts of the 1930s.

Britannia was built in 1893 according to the plans of G. L. Watson for His Royal Highness the Prince of Wales, a keen and able helmsman. From the beginning, *Britannia* was a successful racing yacht, winning races against Kaiser Wilhelm's *Meteors*, among many others. Prince Edward, later to become King Edward VII, was always at the helm. George V, his successor, was also an enthusiastic sailor, and we see him sitting behind the compass surrounded by (from left to right) Sir Fisher Dilke, Michael Mason (owner of *Latifa*), Sir Philip Hunloke at the wheel and Major Towers Clark.

Britannia won over two hundred races in her career – a record that has yet to be surpassed. She was beaten once by *Navahoe*, one of Herreshoff's boats, but fared better against another America's Cup yacht, *Vigilant*, winnng twelve races out of seventeen.

[This photograph shows *Britannia* racing in the Solent off Cowes and just about to complete her two hundredth victory. George V is at the helm.]

When *Britannia* was converted to race in the "J" Class she was stripped of her bulwarks, given a one-piece mast and a bermudian mainsail. And the transition did not interrupt her run of success, although she performed best in hard weather.

Length Overall	102 feet
Waterline length	86 feet
Draft	15 feet
Tonnage	152 tons
Sail Area	11,000 square feet
Hull	Steel
Owner	HM King Edward VII/George V
Designer	G. L. Watson
Builder	D & W Henderson
Built	Clyde, Scotland

Pages 100–101: *Resolute* US Defender (1920)

Herreshoff was once again the designer for the 1920 defender, *Resolute*, though like *Shamrock IV* she had been built for the postponed 1914 series.

She was an extremely light boat with a centreboard to give her an extra seven feet in depth. Her trial horses were *Defiance* and *Vanitie*, and of twenty races she won fifteen.

(Photograph reproduced courtesy of the Rosenfeld Collection Mystic Seaport Museum.)

Length Overall	106 feet 6 inches
Waterline length	75 feet 6 inches
Draft – centreboard	21 feet
Beam	21 feet
Launched	1914
Owner	New York Yacht Club Syndicate
Designer	Nat Herreshoff
Builder	Herreshoff Mfg Co
Built	Bristol, Rhode Island, USA
Skipper	C. F. Adams

Pages 102–103: Charles Nicholson

In this photograph we see Charles Nicholson, designer of many fine yachts, at the wheel of

Candida. The scene is perhaps typical of yachting in the years between the two World Wars: yachting cap, white shirt, club tie and white flannels, all of which were worn by true yachtsmen of the era. To leeward is *Britannia*.

THE "J" CLASS

Over a period of eighty years the long keeled schooners had given way to wide shoal-shaped sloops and cutters, some with centreboards and others with deep keels. All the yachts in this period were elegant, even if they began as sea-going cruisers in the 1850s and ended as racing yachts in the thirties. They were a joy to photograph and every one captures our attention.

When one realizes that there were no winches to haul a great mainsail one hundred feet or more up a mast, or a topsail a further fifty feet, or to haul a great mainsheet in on a gybe from port to starboard, or, indeed, to haul in a boom hanging over the counter by some fifty feet, one begins to understand why it was necessary to have the enormous crews for these boats to carry out manoeuvres smoothly.

Then, in 1930, everything changed. Yachts were to be built under the American Universal Rule Measurement, which ushered in the "J" Class. There was to be a mainsail on a single mast of one hundred and fifty feet or more; a short mainboom, no bowsprits, three headsails, genoa jibs, balloon spinnakers set afore the forestay, Park Avenue booms, steel rod rigging, "coffee grinder" winches and hulls in excess of one hundred and twenty feet, with their interiors not so luxuriously fitted, in order to save weight and make room for winch handling or sail handling under the decks.

And so we enter the "J" class era, when cost seemed immaterial and owners actually took to the helm. Wooden hulls gave way to steel and bronze, and then to aluminium and duraluminium. Older yachts, like *Britannia*, *Astra*, *Candida*, and *Lulworth*, were converted: their bowsprits were shortened, they shed their bulwarks, stripped their hulls and fitted new "Marconi" masts. All the unnecessary furniture went and they joyfully entered the contest. Five "greyhounds" reaching for the line, seconds before the gun, was a sight not to be forgotten.

Pages 106–109: *Shamrock V* **UK Challenger (1930)**

Sir Thomas Lipton launched his fifth challenger, *Shamrock V*, some ten years after his fourth had lost. It had been agreed that the 1930 series should be contested with "J" Class yachts. Now there was to be no more time allowance: the first to cross the line would be the winner. And the design of the "J" Class yachts reflected this change with their limited accommodations and uncluttered decks.

For his challenger, Lipton turned once more to Charles Nicholson, who produced a beautiful sloop. Her launch at the Camper & Nicholson yard in Gosport was quite an event and the photograph on pages 106–107 clearly shows her gleaming hull. It was shamrock green.

Although there were yachts that could give *Shamrock* a good trial in Britain, there were none in the same class. So Lipton took her across the Atlantic hoping to find some suitable opposition before the America's Cup series began.

When the races commenced, *Shamrock* found herself pitted against *Enterprise*, a yacht designed by Starling Burgess. Where Herreshoff had left off, Burgess continued. In the best-of-seven series, *Enterprise* won four, *Shamrock* failing to score a single victory. The margin in the first race was three minutes, in the second it was nine, *Shamrock* retired in the third, and in the fourth it was again nine minutes.

Length Overall	119 feet
Waterline length	81 feet
Beam	20 feet
Draft	14 feet 6 inches
Tonnage	134 tons
Sail Area	7,540 square feet

Owner	Sir Thomas Lipton
Designer	Charles Nicholson
Builder	Camper & Nicholson
Built	Gosport, Hants., England
Hull	Steel, with centreboard
Skipper	E. Heard

Pages 110–111: *Astra* **UK (1930)**

It has been said that some yachts, like some women, inspire an all-transcending love: such was *Astra*. Regarded as one of the most beautiful yachts to be designed by Charles Nicholson, *Astra* always gave a good account of herself in races.

She was slightly smaller than most of her contemporaries, as she had been designed according to the International Rule. In this picture, *Astra* is seen with her wings outspread. As she passed us, we ducked under her boom.

Length Overall	115 feet
Waterline length	75 feet
Beam	20 feet
Draft	13 feet 10 inches
Tonnage	164 tons
Sail Area	7,507 square feet
Owner	Hugh F. Paul
Designer	Charles Nicholson
Builder	Camper & Nicholson
Built	Gosport, Hants., England
Launched	1928

Pages 112–114: *Yankee* **US Defence Candidate (1930)**

Yankee was built in 1930 and raced against *Enterprise*, *Weetamoe* and *Whirlwind* in the US trials for the America's Cup that year. Her hull was of bronze and she had a fin and bulb keel. *Yankee*'s mast soared 150 feet from her deck.

These pictures give a good idea of the length of the "J" Class yachts and also reveal just how finely rigged these boats were. *Yankee*'s double-clewed jib (a sail developed in 1933 by the famous firm Ratsey & Lapthorn of Cowes) can also be seen. This jib stopped the mainsail from being backwinded and allowed the airflow to escape through the lee of the mainsail.

Length Overall	126 feet
Waterline length	83 feet
Beam	22 feet 6 inches
Draft	14 feet 6 inches
Tonnage	148 tons
Designer	Messrs Payne, Belkman & Skene
Builder	G. Lawley & Son
Skipper	J. S. Lawrence
Sail Area	7,300 square feet

Page 115: *Enterprise* **US Defender (1930)**

Harold S. Vanderbilt, head of a New York Yacht Club syndicate, turned to Starling Burgess to design his defender. Burgess duly obliged by producing *Enterprise*, a technologically sophisticated yacht. All round, *Enterprise* was supported by a strong team. She was built at the Herreshoff yard, and in Vanderbilt and Sherman Hoyt she had two formidable helmsmen.

One of Burgess's innovations was to the rig of *Enterprise*: she had a "Park Avenue" boom. This allowed a curve to be put into the foot of the mainsail.

Enterprise may not have beaten *Shamrock V* by vast

margins, but it was generally accepted that she was the better boat and thoroughly deserved her victory.

(*Photograph reproduced courtesy of the Rosenfeld Collection Mystic Seaport Museum*)

Length Overall	120 feet 6 inches
Waterline length	80 feet
Beam	23 feet
Draft	14 feet 6 inches
Hull	Bronze
Owner	New York Yacht Club Syndicate
Designer	W. Starling Burgess
Builder	Herreshoff Mfg Co
Built	Bristol, Rhode Island, USA
Launched	April 1930
Sail Area	7,583 square feet

Pages 116–117: **The Road Behind the Camper & Nicholson Boatyard**

In this evocative photograph we see the bow of *Endeavour* to the left with a ladder leaning against her hull, and her trial horses for the 1934 America's Cup series. From the left: *Shamrock V* is next, followed by *Astra*, *Candida* and *Velsheda*.

Pages 118–119: **UK Trial Horses (1934)**

Velsheda, *Candida*, *Shamrock V*, *Astra* and *Britannia* are lining up at the start of a trial race in this photograph. In fair winds, each of the trialists has its spinnaker up.

Pages 120–121: *Rainbow* **US Defender (1934)**

Rainbow looks the essence of a racing yacht: nearly 130 feet of hull, a forceful bow, a mast of 155 feet, and 7,500 square feet of sail. Once again it was Starling Burgess who was responsible for the classic hull.

The adversaries *Rainbow* was up against were a formidable trio to beat: *Yankee*, *Weetamoe* and *Vanitie*. Among the crew of *Weetamoe* was a young man named Olin Stephens, of the firm Sparkman & Stephens. *Yankee*, however, was her main competition and it was only in the last races that *Rainbow* convinced the committee that she should become the 1934 defender against Sir Thomas Sopwith's *Endeavour*.

The first race started off in a good breeze, with *Rainbow* reaching the first mark a few seconds in front of *Endeavour*, but as they rounded the buoy, *Endeavour* started to pull away and held her lead to the finish, winning by two minutes. The second race saw the challenger pull away from *Rainbow* again; this time she won by fifty seconds. But in the third race *Endeavour*'s fortunes were reversed and *Rainbow* ran out the winner by four minutes. For the next race, which began in a breeze of ten knots, *Rainbow* added two tons of ballast. At the first mark, *Rainbow* found *Endeavour* too close to her lee quarter to round the buoy without fouling the challenger and had to carry on past the mark, letting *Endeavour* take a slight lead. But *Rainbow* came back and eased in front on *Endeavour*'s weather. Sopwith luffed sharply; *Rainbow* did not respond, and the skipper of the challenger raised his protest flag. At the subsequent committee meeting to decide the race it was concluded that Sopwith had not raised his protest flag early enough, so *Rainbow* was awarded the result. The score was now two apiece.

When the fifth race came to be run there was a fresh breeze. *Rainbow* drew ahead, but as she was setting a spinnaker the main boom knocked a crew member overboard. Somehow he managed to grasp hold of a back stay and was pulled aboard. The incident could have been far worse and *Rainbow* might have lost the race, but as it turned out she went on to win by four minutes. At the start of the sixth race, both boats were circling, waiting for the off. *Endeavour* found herself forty seconds ahead, but as the two boats tacked, *Rainbow* came through to win the race by fifty-five seconds, and thus took the series by four races to two.

Length Overall	127 feet 6 inches
Waterline length	82 feet
Beam	21 feet
Draft	15 feet
Tonnage	141 tons
Sail Area	7,535 square feet
Owner	New York Yacht Club Syndicate (Vanderbilt)
Designer	W. Starling Burgess
Builder	Herreshoff Co.
Built	Bristol, Rhode Island, USA
Launched	1934
Hull	Steel topside, bronze underwater

Pages 122–123: *Velsheda* **UK Trial Horse (1934)**

Velsheda, a cutter built in 1933, was owned by the then Director of Woolworths, who had his eye on an America's Cup challenge. She raced against *Endeavour I* and *II* in Britain, but both of these were faster than *Velsheda* in every respect.

The photograph on page 123 was taken in 1934 and shows *Velsheda* in the heyday of her racing life, carrying the spinnaker that was then fashionable – the holes were intended to keep the sail filled at all times, working on the same principle as a parachute.

Velsheda withstood the test of time. This year, 1990, she will be still cruising British waters. Her name, by the way, is derived from the names of the owner's three daughters: Velma, Sheila and Daphne.

Length Overall	127 feet 6 inches
Waterline length	83 feet
Beam	21 feet 6 inches
Draft	15 feet
Hull	Steel
Sail Area	7,542 square feet
Owner	W. L. Stephenson
Designer	Charles Nicholson
Builder	Camper & Nicholson
Built	Gosport, Hants., England
Launched	1933

Pages 124–125: *Endeavour* UK Challenger (1934)

Sir Thomas Sopwith, the owner of *Endeavour*, was no stranger to the sea. He had raced in small boats for a long time and between 1927 and 1930 he won the Twelve Metre championships in Britain. Sopwith was familiar with the "J" Class yachts as he had bought *Shamrock V* after Sir Thomas Lipton's death. *Endeavour* was designed by Charles Nicholson and had a shiny blue hull.

When *Endeavour* reached America, Sopwith arranged several races against *Vanitie* so as to get his challenger into shape for the forthcoming series. On board as regular crew were the designer, Nicholson, and Sopwith's wife.

It has already been said that *Endeavour* won the first two races and *Rainbow* the third. Then there was the controversial fourth race, when Sopwith luffed and then bore away to avoid a collision that might well have endangered both crews. The committee's decision in favour of the defender marred an otherwise closely fought series.

In recent times *Endeavour* has been completely restored by Elizabeth Meyer, and in 1989 she sailed into Cowes the picture of yachting perfection. It had been fifty years since I had last photographed her. Now, after being restored by a Dutch firm and fitted

with canvas made by Hood Sails of Italy, she flies the American flag.

Length Overall	129 feet 6 inches
Waterline length	83 feet 6 inches
Beam	22 feet
Draft	14 feet 9 inches
Hull	Steel
Tonnage	143 tons
Sail Area	7,561 square feet
Owner	Sir Thomas Sopwith, R.Y.S.
Designer	Charles Nicholson
Builder	Camper & Nicholson
Built	Gosport, Hants., England
Launched	1934
Skipper	Sir Thomas Sopwith

Page 126: *Endeavour II* UK Challenger (1937)

Once more Charles Nicholson was invited by Sir Thomas Sopwith to design the challenger. It had been generally accepted that in the previous series *Endeavour I* was a faster yacht than *Rainbow*, even if she hadn't won the cup. *Endeavour II* was a bigger boat altogether, so as to reach the maximum limit for waterline length under "J" Class rules.

Sopwith took both *Endeavour*s across the Atlantic in order to give the challenger time to adapt to local conditions with a perfect trial horse. In all, there were one hundred and one tests in all weathers: sail handling tests and start practices, all geared to making the second *Endeavour* a thoroughbred.

Ranger defended the cup, and a redoubtable yacht she was too. The first race began with each boat splitting tacks with the other so as not to become pinned down. But *Ranger* pulled away and at the end of the course found herself seventeen minutes in front of the challenger. The second race was a repeat performance, with *Ranger* winning by fifteen minutes. The third was slightly tighter, but the defender still led by four minutes. After having won two races in the 1934 series, it looked as if Sopwith was not going to win even one in 1937. Which was

exactly what happened. In the final race, *Ranger* pulled away and confirmed her superiority by winning with three and a half minutes to spare.

Length Overall	135 feet 6 inches
Waterline length	87 feet
Beam	21 feet 6 inches
Draft	15 feet
Hull	Steel
Tonnage	162½ tons
Sail Area	7,543 square feet
Owner	Sir Thomas Sopwith, R.Y.S.
Designer	Charles Nicholson
Builder	Camper & Nicholson
Built	Gosport, Hants., England
Launched	1936
Skipper	Sir Thomas Sopwith

Page 127: *Ranger* US Defender (1937)

If Charles Nicholson was responsible for all the challengers of the 1930s, Starling Burgess was responsible for all the defenders – except that for the 1937 series he teamed up with Olin Stephens and the Sparkman & Stephens firm. There were six designs for the new defender, all of which were subjected to rigorous tank testing at the Stevens Institute in New Jersey. Models of two previous defenders, *Enterprise* and *Rainbow*, were also made, along with the previous challenger, *Endeavour I*. *Ranger* emerged from these sophisticated tests as an outstanding prospect. After she was launched it soon became clear that all the tank and wind tunnel testing had produced excellent results. In the trials she defeated *Rainbow* and *Yankee*, and in Vanderbilt, his wife, Olin Stephens and Arthur Knapp, they had a tremendous crew.

Ranger had some problems with her rigging early in the season. One must appreciate that with a mast of over one hundred and fifty feet careful support rigging was fundamental. A vast area of sail had to be supported in all conditions.

At the end of the series, Olin Stephens was at the helm. We shall be hearing much more about the Sparkman & Stephens firm in challenges to come.

(Photograph reproduced courtesy of the Rosenfeld Collection Mystic Seaport Museum. Acquired in honour of Franz Schneider.)

Length Overall	135 feet
Waterline length	87 feet
Beam	21 feet
Draft	15 feet
Hull	Steel
Sail Area	7,546 square feet
Owner	Harold S. Vanderbilt
Designer	W. Starling Burgess, Sparkman & Stephens
Builder	Bath Ironworks
Built	Bath, Maine, USA

THE TWELVE METRE CLASS

If ever there was a sporting event guaranteed to be a funnel for tens of thousands of pounds it was the contest between two "J" Class yachts for one trophy. The names of those big boats, as well as the notable gentlemen who participated, are an enduring memory in the minds of most sailors today. But the "J" Class will also be remembered for bringing an accepted measurement unity which was to last until 1988.

The Second World War put paid to the "J"s and that era of opulent racing. It was not until 1946 that the British suggested another challenge and it was a further ten years before negotiations were concluded over the dimensions of the yachts that were to race. Smaller yachts were the result: the Twelve Metre Class. Considerably cheaper to build than the "J" Class yachts of the thirties, they were an acceptable craft with which to champion a nation's pride. Ten matches were to be held over the next thirty years.

If the Twelves had been chosen in 1956 for the cheapness with which they could be built, by the seventies and eighties America's Cup racing, and spending, had changed out of all recognition. Millions of pounds, dollars, francs, and lire were being put into designing the latest yachts. The opulent thirties had returned.

Pages 130–31: *Flica II* UK (1958)

Flica II was a twelve metre yacht built before the Second World War and was to compete against two British challengers. She was designed by Laurent Giles and built in Fairlie, Scotland.

In the photograph on page 131, *Flica II* can be seen travelling fast with her crew well outboard.

Length Overall	67 feet
Waterline length	46 feet
Draft	9 feet 6 inches
Owner	Jack Salem
Designer	Laurent Giles
Built	Fairlie, Scotland

Page 132: *Sceptre* UK Challenger (1958)

Sceptre was the first of two designs by David Boyd and the first twelve metre to challenge for the cup. She underwent exhaustive sea trials in the Solent to prepare for the America's Cup races.

Sceptre was unusual in that she had a deep open cockpit so that all sheeting and winching was worked well below deck. In the trial races against *Flica II*, *Evaine* and *Kaylena*, I was asked aboard to film the gybing and the hoisting and lowering of the spinnaker, to ensure that these manoeuvres were

being carried out with the maximum speed. The huge French spinnaker, the Herbulot, made its first appearance in these races.

Sceptre was shipped over to New York and the first race commenced on 20 September. It was soon clear that the defender, *Columbia*, was pulling away from *Sceptre* with each tack. She led round each mark and finished seven minutes in front. In the second race, *Columbia* increased the margin between the two boats at the finish to eleven minutes, and to eight minutes in the third. In the fourth, *Sceptre* crossed the line before the gun and had to return to re-cross. This put the defender well into the lead and the race seemed an assured American victory when *Sceptre's* mainsail boom broke. The British boat managed to continue, and although she lost by seven minutes she acquitted herself well; but she was a poor performer in almost all conditions and never really stood a chance.

Length Overall	68 feet 6 inches
Waterline length	46 feet 6 inches
Draft	9 feet
Sail Area	1,832 square feet
Hull	Wood
Launched	1958
Owner	Syndicate (H. Goodson, Viscount Runciman etc.)
Designer	David Boyd
Builder	Alex Robertson
Built	Sandbank, Holy Loch, Scotland
Skipper	Graham Mann

Pages 133: Twelve Metre *Columbia* US Defender (1958)

Olin Stephens designed the defender for 1958 and brought all his vast experience to bear in the design of *Columbia*. Rigging is an important factor, as much as the design of the hull, and it can be seen that *Columbia* had two sets of spreaders on her mast. For her sheeting, two "coffee grinder" winches were well placed on deck.

Columbia's rivals were *Easterner*, designed by Ray Hunt, and *Weatherly*, designed by Phil Rhodes, as well as Olin Stephens' *Vim*. Inevitably, *Columbia* ran out the winner.

Morris Rosenfeld very kindly took me out to cover the first race (his camera was almost as ancient as mine) and we saw *Columbia* win in light winds.

Length Overall	69 feet 8 inches
Waterline length	45 feet 10 inches
Draft	9 feet
Sail Area	1,846 square feet
Hull	Wood
Launched	1958
Owner	Syndicate (Henry, Briggs Cunningham etc.)

Designer	Olin J. Stephens
Builder	Nevins Yacht Yard
Built	City Island, NY, USA
Skipper	Briggs S. Cunningham

Page 134: *Gretel* Australian Challenger (1962)

The eighteenth challenge for the America's Cup came from Australia. *Gretel*, built for Sir Frank Packer and designed by Alan Payne, was one of the first twelve metre yachts to be made in Australia. Sir Frank chartered *Vim* in order to give his challenger a good trial horse.

The first cup race was an exciting event with *Weatherly* sailing as defender. The breeze should have helped *Gretel*, but she could not hold *Weatherly* and finished three minutes behind. *Gretel* came back in the second, however, and won by forty-one seconds – a victory due to the sail handling of her crew as much as anything else.

With one race each it looked as though the series might be close, but in the third *Weatherly* finished over eight minutes in front. *Gretel* lost again in the fourth, if only by eleven seconds, and in the fifth

could not find the speed to match the defender, who went on to win by a comfortable three minutes and forty-five seconds.

Length Overall	69 feet 6 inches
Waterline length	46 feet 2½ inches
Sail Area	1,854 square feet
Hull	Wood
Draft	9 feet
Launched	1962
Owner	Sir Frank Packer Syndicate
Designer	Alan Payne
Builder	Lars Halvorsen & Sons
Built	Ryde, Australia
Skipper	A. S. Sturrock

Page 135: *Weatherly* US Defender (1962)

In these great challenges it is easy to forget the fundamental role of the designers and the helmsmen. *Weatherly* was designed by Philip Rhodes and had "Bus" Mosbacher as helmsman – a formidable team. Mosbacher had been sailing Six Metre yachts for some time. It was his brilliant tactics that secured *Weatherly's* victory.

Length Overall	67 feet
Waterline length	45 feet 6 inches
Hull	Wood
Draft	9 feet
Sail Area	1,840 square feet
Launched	1958
Owner	New York Yacht Club Syndicate
Designer	Philip L. Rhodes
Builder	Luders Marine Co
Built	Stamford, Conn., USA
Skipper	Bus Mosbacher

Pages 136–137: *American Eagle* US Defence Candidate (1964)

There were two contenders for the defence of the America's Cup in 1964, *American Eagle* and

Constellation. Throughout the season both yachts had systematically beaten the older twelves and both were evenly matched, although on many occasions *American Eagle* had the upper hand. Luck was not with her when it counted, however, and it was *Constellation* who was selected. *American Eagle's* helmsman, Bill Cox, could content himself with the fact that although *Constellation* had proved to have greater potential, he had inflicted several battle scars on the defender.

American Eagle went on to make a bid for the defence in 1967, racing against *Intrepid*, and then had a spell in Australia, where she paced *Gretel II*. Subsequently she was converted to race offshore and was to become famous as an ocean "greyhound", setting a new record for the Fastnet race in 1971 of three days, seven hours eleven minutes and forty-eight seconds.

Length Overall	68 feet
Waterline length	46 feet 7 inches
Hull	Wood
Draft	9 feet 1 inch
Sail Area	1,850 square feet
Launched	1964
Owner	Aurora Syndicate
Designer	A. E. Luders
Builder	Luders Marine Co
Built	Stamford, Conn. USA
Skipper	W. S. Cox

Page 138: *Sovereign* UK Challenger (1964)

Once more it was David Boyd who designed the next challenger and *Sovereign* was the result. She was not very different from most conventional twelve metre yachts. Peter Scott took the helm – a surprise to many, as he had not raced in this class to any extent, or in anything else in recent years for that matter.

Sovereign's trials with *Sceptre* proved disappointing, so Boyd designed another very similar twelve metre, *Kurrewa*, to give his new challenger some stiffer opposition. Meanwhile, another syndicate had re-built the pre-war *Norsaga*, hoping that she would sail against the America's Cup defender. There was therefore good competition.

Out of these demanding trials *Sovereign* emerged as the best of the three, even if the final trials had taken place in America against *Kurrewa*.

The British challenger was up against a tough defender, *Constellation*, who pulled away from *Sovereign* at the start of the first race and extended her lead to five and a half minutes by the finish. In the second, *Constellation* won by twenty minutes, and in the third by six and a half minutes. Finally, she

finished fifteen minutes ahead in the fourth to take the Cup.

Length Overall	69 feet
Waterline length	46 feet
Hull	Wood
Draft	9 feet
Sail Area	1,876 square feet
Launched	1963
Owner	Anthony J. Boyden, RTYC
Designer	David Boyd
Builder	Alex Robertson
Built	Sandbanks, Holy Loch, Scotland
Skipper	Peter Scott

Page 139: *Constellation* US Defender (1964)

Constellation was the work of Olin Stephens, his third America's Cup defender. As trial horse and rivals she had *Columbia*, *American Eagle*, and *Nefertiti* – the latter a 1962 Ted Hood design. Weight saving was now the name of the game – hull and rigging had to be as light as possible – and *Constellation* was designed with this consideration in mind.

The trials were especially tough, but *Constellation*, with Bob Bavier at the helm and Rod Stephens aboard, came through to become the defender. These rigorous trials were particularly helpful in ensuring *Constellation's* victory over *Sovereign*.

Length Overall	68 feet 4 inches
Waterline length	46 feet 5 inches
Hull	Wood
Draft	9 feet 1 inch
Sail Area	1,818 square feet
Launched	1964
Owner	New York Yacht Club Syndicate
Designer	Olin J. Stephens
Builder	Minneford Yacht Yard
Built	City Island, NY, USA
Skipper	R. N. Bavier

Page 140: *Dame Pattie* Australian Challenger (1967)

In order to comply with the new New York Yacht Club rules that each challenger be entirely "home grown", Australia turned to Warwick Hood for the design of *Dame Pattie*. *Gretel*, who had benefitted from American technology but had been built prior to the introduction of this clause, was also in the running after major surgery, but *Dame Pattie* established herself as the only real contender for the challenge. She was helped by the use of a new sailcloth (developed by Joe Pearce and said to be stronger than the American-produced Dacron) and a highly determined crew.

When *Dame Pattie* was confronted by the defender, *Intrepid*, skipper Jock Sturrock knew that the Australian team had their work cut out for them if they were to put up an honourable challenge. This proved to be so; *Intrepid* won four easy races. Only in the second – and then only shortly – did *Dame Pattie* find herself in the lead.

The Australians returned a little deflated, but *Dame Pattie* was to serve well as an Australian trial horse in years to come, before being converted for offshore racing.

(Photograph reproduced courtesy of the Rosenfeld Collection Mystic Seaport Museum.)

Length Overall	65 feet 1 inch
Waterline length	47 feet
Hull	Wood
Draft	9 feet 2 inches
Sail Area	1,761 square feet
Launched	1966
Owner	Royal Sydney Yacht Squadron Syndicate
Designer	Warwick J. Hood
Builder	William Barnet Co
Built	Sydney, Australia
Skipper	Jock Sturrock

Page 141: *Intrepid* US Defender (1967)

The talent and experience of the Americans for twelve metre racing were now vast and they also had a sizable fleet with which to experiment. Even so, with the ever increasing strength of the challengers it was felt that the design of America's Cup yachts needed an injection of fresh thinking, and Olin Stephens was to begin a new chapter with *Intrepid*.

The rudder of his new boat was placed well aft behind a full bustle running from the keel, where a large vertical trim-tab acted as the trailing edge. All this provided upwind lift. Also, there was a low deck-sweeping boom; with the crew and their winches well below deck level, *Intrepid's* centre of gravity was remarkably low. To race against his new yacht in the trials, Olin Stephens radically altered *Columbia*, though this did not include the introduction of a separate rudder.

The Americans were confident they had a very strong defender and the four America's Cup races matched their expectations. *Intrepid* never won by less than three and a half minutes.

(Photograph reproduced courtesy of the Rosenfeld Collection Mystic Seaport Museum.)

Length Overall	64 feet 3 inches
Waterline length	46 feet 10 inches
Hull	Wood
Draft	9 feet 1 inch
Sail Area	1,757 square feet
Launched	1967
Owner	New York Yacht Club Syndicate
Designer	Olin J. Stephens
Builder	Minneford Yacht Yard
Built	City Island, NY, USA
Skipper	E. Mosbacher

Page 142: *Gretel II* Australian Challenger (1970)

The Australians had been disappointed by *Gretel's* performance. In 1970 Sir Frank Packer asked designer, Alan Payne, to sweep the board with a new challenger. Payne responded with *Gretel II*, which incorporated several innovative ideas. She had twin steering wheels and collapsible spreaders, and her large bustle extended to a shortened keel filled with an oversize trim-tab.

In the challengers' trials, *Gretel II* had to race against *France*, owned by Baron Bich, before she could go on to contest the cup itself. To ensure that his boat was as finely tuned as possible Sir Frank had chartered *American Eagle*, an earlier defence candidate, and this certainly helped. *France* was beaten and *Gretel II* went through to make the challenge.

In the first cup race *Gretel II* snapped a spinnaker pole and then lost a man overboard. The defender,

the redesigned *Intrepid*, finished five minutes in front. Just as *Gretel II* was proving a match for *Intrepid* in the second race, fog led to its cancellation. When the race was re-run, *Gretel II* finished first, but a questionable luff at the start had led to a collision and an American protest. *Intrepid* was awarded the race. The third race was again won by *Intrepid*, but in the fourth *Gretel II* demonstrated what a fine yacht she was and beat the defender. Australian joy, however, was short lived. In the last race of the series *Intrepid* won by one and three quarter minutes to retain the cup. The Australians returned home in the knowledge that they had designed a fast boat and if only their racing tactics had been better they might have won.

Length Overall	62 feet 3 inches
Waterline length	47 feet 7 inches
Hull	Wood
Draft	9 feet 3 inches
Sail Area	1,755 square feet
Launched	1970
Owner	Frank Packer Syndicate
	Royal Sydney Yacht Squadron
Designer	Alan Payne
Builder	W. H. Barnett Co
Built	Sydney, Australia
Skipper	J. G. Hardy

Page 143: *Intrepid* US Defender (1970)

Britton Chance was invited to re-design *Intrepid* after successfully building a French twelve metre, *Chancegger*. Olin Stephens was working on a new boat of his own, *Valiant*, and in addition there was Charles Morgan's *Heritage*. The defenders' trials would be keenly fought this year.

Chance's aim was to improve *Intrepid*'s performance in strong winds. He set the rudder further aft on a lengthened bustle and gave her a fuller hull, so that she had a greater waterline length and displaced an extra two and a half tons. With many changes to the rigging and sail plans, *Intrepid* emerged a new boat. But in the trials it was not clear if she was any faster than she had been in 1967.

In the end she saw off *Valiant*, her main rival, and with Bill Ficker and his crew *Intrepid* went into the cup races the favourite to retain the America's Cup. The Australian boat *Gretel II* was, however, a strong contender and the American margin of victory in each race was narrow (never more than one and three quarter minutes). The Australians were learning!

(*Photograph reproduced courtesy of Rosenfeld Collection Mystic Seaport Museum.*)

Length Overall	64 feet 3 inches
Waterline length	48 feet 4 inches
Hull	Wood
Draft	9 feet 4 inches
Sail Area	1,720 square feet
Launched	1967
Owner	Bartram/Strawbridge Syndicate
Designer	Olin Stephens/Britton Chance
Builder	Minneford Yacht Yard
Built	City Island, NY, USA
Skipper	W. P. Ficker

Page 144: *Southern Cross* Australian Challenger (1974)

New rule changes established a challengers' competiton to be contested in the same waters that the cup races were to be fought; prospective challengers could come from any yacht club in any country. The rules had been altered mainly because seven challenges were lodged after the 1970 competition, although external influences such as the oil crisis combined with new design factors (such as the legality of aluminium hulls) narrowed the eventual number of challenges down to two: *France II* and *Southern Cross*.

Alan Bond, of the Royal Perth Yacht Club, had purchased Sir Frank Packer's two boats, *Gretel I* and *II*,

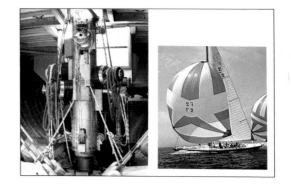

and had commissioned Bob Miller to design a faster yacht to outpace them. So emerged *Southern Cross*.

In the trials at Newport, Rhode Island, the initial battle was fought in the club house. Baron Bich had commissioned the Danish champion skipper, Paul Elvstrom, to build a new yacht, *France II*, but Bich was unhappy with the design and therefore decided to race his earlier boat, *France I*, instead. (*France I* had in fact sunk under tow, but was recovered in time to race.) Despite these complications, *Southern Cross* emerged as the challenger.

The Australians firmly believed that they would be up against an inferior defender: they could not have been more wrong. *Courageous* took the first race by nearly five minutes. The second was closer, but in the third (re-run after fog intervened) the Americans won most convincingly. In the fourth and final race *Courageous* crossed the finishing line over seven minutes ahead of her rival.

(*Photograph reproduced courtesy of the Rosenfeld Collection Mystic Seaport Museum.*)

Length Overall	67 feet 3 inches
Waterline length	46 feet 8 inches
Hull	Aluminium
Draft	9 feet 1 inch
Sail Area	1,811 square feet
Launched	1974
Owner	Alan Bond, Royal Perth
	Yacht Club
Designer	Bob Miller
Builder	Halvorsen, Morson & Gowland
Built	Terry Hills, NSW, Australia
Skipper	Jim Hardy

Page 145: *Courageous* US Defender (1974)

Not since the selection trials between *Vim* and *Columbia* had two boats fought on such equal terms as *Courageous* and *Intrepid*. In addition, there were other candidates: Britton Chance's *Mariner* and the old *Valiant* who (despite the work of George Hinman and Ted Turner) failed to show the necessary speed to keep up with the newer boats. *Mariner*, with Dennis Conner at the helm, was not a match for the three Stephens-designed yachts. She had a radical tumblehome hull, a bulbous underwater bow section and a fin rudder, but even these features were not enough to keep her in the running.

Intrepid had been extensively re-modelled by Olin Stephens and had surpassed her 1967 performance level. Skippered by Gerry Driscoll, she gave *Courageous* (who numbered Bob Bavier and Ted Hood among her crew) a fine run for her money and it was not until the final eliminator races that *Courageous* came out in front.

After the hotly contested defenders' trials the cup races were an anti-climax. *Courageous* won in four straight races.

Length Overall	65 feet 11 inches
Waterline length	45 feet 3 inches
Draft	8 feet 10 inches
Hull	Aluminium
Sail Area	1,772 square feet
Launched	1974
Owner	New York Yacht Club Syndicate
Designer	Sparkman & Stephens
Builder	Minneford Yacht Yard
Built	City Island, NY, USA
Skipper	Ted Hood

Pages 146–147: *France II* French Challenger Candidate (1977)

The second French challenger for the America's Cup was sponsored by Baron Marcel Bich of the Yacht Club d'Hyeres. Designed by Andre Mauric and built by the Chantier AFCA, Hermann Egger, *France II* featured a mast stepped on rubber and with a mechanical fitting to the deckhead, which allowed the mast to be angled in various positions while racing. Her challenge was to prove unsuccessful; she was eliminated during the selection trials and *Australia* went on to race against the American defender that year.

Length Overall	63 feet 5 inches
Waterline length	47 feet 6 inches
Draft	9 feet 2½ inches
Sail Area	1,840 square feet
Owner	Baron Marcel Bich
Beam	12 feet 8 inches
Tonnage	28.8 tons
Hull	Wood

Page 148: *Australia* Australian Challenger (1977)

There were new safety regulations for the 1977 series which included rulings on hatches and the size of self-draining cockpits. Potential challengers that year included *Sverige*, *France I* and *France II*, while the Australians brought a much altered *Gretel II* and a new aluminium hulled yacht, *Australia*. Britain's hopefuls, alas, failed to materialize.

France II had been extensively reworked without her original designer's approval, but she was no match for her younger competitors and was soon eliminated. The final selection trials therefore featured *Gretel II*, *Sverige* and *Australia*.

The Australians were learning from their hard fought lessons, and with *Australia* had a lighter and smaller twelve metre, eminently suitable for the light winds off Newport. Four straight losses put the Swedes out of the challenge and *Australia* went on to decide the America's Cup against *Courageous*.

The Americans did not lose a race. Although *Australia* showed she had speed, she could not point as high as *Courageous* and lost out on the up-wind legs. But the gap between defender and challenger was closing, and Australian confidence, despite this setback, remained high.

Length Overall	64 feet 5 inches
Waterline length	45 feet
Draft	8 feet 10 inches
Sail Area	1,801 square feet
Hull	Aluminium

Launched	1977
Owner	Alan Bond, W Australia Syndicate
Designer	J. Valentijn/B. Lexcen
Built	Perth, Australia
Skipper	Noel Robbins

Page 149: *Courageous* US Defender (1977)

The 1977 America's Cup saw the USA do all they could to ensure a successful defence. Three boats emerged in the front line: *Enterprise* was the new Sparkman & Stephens design for Edward Du Moulin's New York Yacht Club syndicate, skippered by Lowell North and with *Intrepid* for a stable-mate; *Independence* was Ted Hood's creation for the Alfred Loomis syndicate; and *Courageous*, the previous defender, helped *Independence* to prepare for the trials and was brought in as a contender in her own right at Ted Turner's insistence.

Turner proved to be right: *Courageous* dominated the trials, and Turner's skills as helmsman played no small part in this success. So *Courageous* joined that illustrious elite of two-time America's Cup defenders (her predecessors were *Columbia* in 1899 and 1901, and *Intrepid* in 1967 and 1970). Furthermore she defended in style, despatching *Australia* without losing a single race.

Length Overall	65 feet 11 inches
Waterline length	44 feet 9 inches
Draft	8 feet 10 inches
Hull	Aluminium
Sail Area	1,772 square feet
Built	1974
Owner	Ted Turner & Syndicate
Designer	Olin Stephens
Builder	Minneford Yacht Yard
Built	City Island, NY, USA
Skipper	Ted Turner

Page 150: *Lionheart* UK Challenge Candidate (1980)

Lionheart came to the 1980 America's Cup challengers' trials as the winner of the first World Championships in 1979. She had practised with two previous American defenders, *Constellation* and *Columbia*.

Lionheart, designed by Ian Howlett, was a heavy yacht and, as the photograph shows, she had a highly flexible mast; without infringing the rules, this gave her an added sixty square feet of sail area and a more efficient airflow. The British challenger was to lose in a series of gallantly fought races against *France III*.

Length Overall	64 feet
Waterline length	47 feet 7 inches
Draft	9 feet 2 inches
Hull	Aluminium
Sail Area	1,825 square feet
Owner	British Industry 1500 Syndicate
Designer	Ian Howlett
Builder	Joyce Marine
Skipper	Lawrie Smith
Built	1979

Page 151: *Freedom* US Defender (1980)

Olin Stephens has an assured place in the history of the America's Cup. In 1934 he was aboard *Weetamoe*

as a crew member; in 1937 he and his firm, Sparkman & Stephens, contributed to the design of the successful defender, *Ranger*. Thereafter he dominated the defence of the America's Cup with yachts such as *Courageous* and *Intrepid*, two boats who defended the cup on more than one occasion.

Freedom was his design for the 1980 defence and she dominated the trials. Even the sterling efforts of *Courageous* could do little to prevent *Freedom* from winning thirty-six of the forty races in which she competed. The most salient feature of Stephens' new Twelve Metre was her low centre of gravity, which allowed her to perform well in strong winds.

She was a strong defender, which she needed to be as the Australian challenger that year had showed considerable potential. Yet *Freedom*, skippered by Dennis Conner in his first America's Cup defence, lost only one race – the second – and proved herself the better yacht overall.

(*Photograph reproduced courtesy of the Rosenfeld Collection Mystic Seaport Museum.*)

Length Overall	63 feet 2 inches
Waterline length	45 feet 8 inches
Beam	12 feet 3 inches
Sail Area	1,800 square feet
Owner	New York Yacht Club Syndicate
Designer	Sparkman & Stephens
Skipper	Dennis Conner

Pages 152–153: *Australia* Australian Challenger (1980)

Australia came to the 1980 America's Cup challenge having been extensively reworked by Ben Lexcen, her designer. Jim Hardy was her skipper and John Bertrand the tactician. In the first round of selection trials *Australia* had a tough battle with the re-worked *Sverige* – in one race her mast broke, though that particular contest was subsequently declared void after a protest was lodged. She then proceeded, in the next round, to take on *France III*, owned by Baron Bich (this was to be his last America's Cup challenger), designed by Valentijn and skippered by Bruno Trouble. After five races, *Australia* qualified as challenger.

Freedom was the boat the Australians had to beat; to this end they had adapted *Australia* so that, like *Lionheart*, she had a flexible mast and thus greater sail area and more lift. The challenger lost the first race, possibly because the crew were unfamiliar with their new rig, but in a re-run second race *Australia* won by half a minute. She seemed a faster yacht in light winds and gave the Americans cause for concern.

Australian hopes were short-lived, however. The next three races were won by *Freedom*, but Alan Bond was convinced that all he needed was one more try to successfully spirit the America's Cup away to Australia.

Length Overall	64 feet 5 inches
Waterline length	45 feet
Draft	8 feet 10 inches
Sail Area	1,801 square feet
Hull	Aluminium
Launched	1977
Owner	Alan Bond, W Australia Syndicate

Designer	J. Valentijn/B. Lexcen
Builder	S. Ward & B. Raley
Built	Perth, Australia
Skipper	Jim Hardy

Pages 154 and 156–157: *Australia II* Australian Challenger (1983)

For the seventh Australian attempt at the America's Cup, Alan Bond turned once more to Ben Lexcen for the design of a new Twelve Metre. Using Dutch tank-testing facilities, Lexcen came up with *Australia II*. She had a short waterline length, small bustle, large sail area and, above all, a revolutionary wing keel.

There were other Australian challengers: *Challenge 12*, also a Lexcen design, was entered by Richard Pratt; and *Advance*, built for Syd Fisher to an Alan Payne design. The British arrived at Newport with *Victory '82*, designed by Ed Dubois, and Ian Howlett's *Victory*, while the French returned with *France III*. There was also a Canadian challenge – *Canada 1* – and a first Italian appearance with *Azzura*.

There was no question as to the best performer in the selection races for challenger: out of fifty-four races, *Australia II* won forty-eight. These lengthy trials gave her tremendous experience for the cup races. Her wing keel, which had been kept secret for so long, became the target of American protests. It was claimed that it infringed the rules governing

draft and should therefore be outlawed. The protest was not upheld by the governing committee.

The first race went to the Americans and *Liberty*, skippered by Dennis Conner. The defender also won the second race after *Australia II*'s mainsail car broke at the top of the mast after the start. Colin Beashel was hoisted up the mast to repair the damage. *Australia II* won the third in a re-run: time had expired on the first attempt with the Australians only just short of the finish. This three minute win and the lead gained when race three was first run showed that the Australians had an edge over *Liberty* in light winds, giving the Americans cause for concern. Conner took the next race to give *Liberty* a two race lead, but *Australia II* won the fifth (probably aided by a rigging failure on *Liberty*) and then the sixth. Never before had an America's Cup series been so closely fought. The whole world waited with bated breath for the final race to begin. The two skippers, John Bertrand and Dennis Conner, both raced superbly, but *Australia II* performed impeccably to take the race by forty-one seconds. The Cup was Australia's at last.

Length Overall	63 feet
Waterline length	43 feet
Draft	8 feet 6 inches
Sail Area	1,830 square feet
Hull	Aluminium
Launched	1977
Owner	Alan Bond
Designer	Ben Lexcen
Builder	S Ward Co
Built	Perth, Australia
Skipper	John Bertrand

Page 155: *Liberty* US Defender (1983)

Five boats were engaged for the twenty-fifth defence. Chuck Kirsch led a syndicate that re-modelled *Courageous* and commissioned a new Twelve, *Defender*, designed by Dave Pedrick. The Freedom Campaign '83 syndicate built *Spirit of America*, a yacht with a heavy displacement designed by Bill Langan of Sparkman & Stephens, as well as a lighter Valentijn design, *Magic*. When it was clear that neither of these boats were performing well, Valentijn was commissioned to produce a new boat, which was named *Liberty*. She was more conservative than *Magic* and *Spirit of America* and after many alterations became the yacht for Dennis Conner, who had established himself as the best skipper afloat. *Liberty* had a further strength in that she had three measurement certificates. By altering sail area and ballast accordingly she could be measured as a Twelve Metre to suit all weather conditions. Depending on the forecast she could alter her trim to suit the day.

The selection trials for the defence were a demonstration of Conner's skills and *Liberty*'s potential. *Courageous* showed that she was still among the best and was runner-up, ahead of *Defender*. The latter had been cut in half, shortened and re-welded so as to reduce her waterline, thus allowing an extra forty square feet of sail.

In the most dramatic of America's Cup competitions, *Liberty* took the first race, but Conner was well aware of *Australia II*'s tacking ability and duels were avoided if at all possible. Moreover, even if the Americans had the better skipper, the Australians certainly had the superior boat. In the extraordinary seventh and final race, Conner won the start, then let Bertrand and *Australia II* take the lead briefly before going ahead at the first mark. At the last mark *Liberty* had slipped and lay twenty-one seconds behind. The last beat saw *Liberty* engaged in tack after tack, as Conner desperately tried to catch up with the challenger. But Bertrand covered well, refusing to let the defender through and so went on to win the most famous race since *America* had won the Hundred Guinea Cup in 1851.

(Photograph used courtesy of the Rosenfeld Collection Mystic Seaport Museum.)

Length Overall	63 feet 6 inches
Waterline length	44 feet 8 inches
Draft	8 feet 9 inches
Hull	Aluminium
Sail Area	1,800 square feet
Launched	1983
Owner	Freedom Campaign '83
Designer	J. Valentijn
Builder	Newport Offshore
Built	Rhode Island, USA
Skipper	Dennis Conner

Page 158: *Australia II* and *New Zealand* (1987)

In this photograph, taken at the 1986 World Championships held at Perth, *New Zealand* holds off *Australia II*, "the little White Pointer". In the defence trials for the 1987 America's Cup, *Australia II*, still dear to the hearts of all Aussies, was to be outclassed by her newer rivals.

New Zealand was to reach the finals of the challengers' competition but eventually lost to Dennis Conner in *Stars & Stripes*.

New Zealand	
Length Overall	19.5 metres

Waterline length	14.1 metres
Draft	2.70 metres
Hull	G.R.P.
Launched	1986
Owner	BNZ Americas Cup Challenge
Designer	B. Farr, R. Holland & L. Davidson
Builder	McMullen & Wing/Marten Marine
Skipper	Chris Dickson

Page 159: *Azzura* Italian Challenge Candidate (1987)

Azzura was the first Italian yacht to challenge for the America's Cup, an attempt led by the Aga Khan and Gianni Agnelli. She sailed under the Yacht Club Costa Emerelda and was launched in 1982. Designed by Vallicelli, she gave a creditable performance in 1983 and established Italy as a main contender to challenge for the cup in years to come.

Length Overall	65 feet 7 inches
Waterline length	45 feet 6 inches
Draft	8 feet 11 inches
Sail Area	1,796 square feet
Hull	Aluminium
Owner	Sfida Italiana
Designer	A. Vallicelli
Builder	Officina Meccanica Ing.
Skipper	Cino Ricci
Launched	1977

Pages 160–161: Group of Twelve Metre Yachts at Perth 1986

As a precursor to the first America's Cup to be contested out of American waters, there was the World Championships held at Perth in 1986. Fourteen of the finest Twelve Metre yachts the world could muster came together to compete. In this picture we see four yachts rushing downwind off the coast of Western Australia.

Pages 162–163: *Italia* Italian Challenge Candidate (1987)

Italia was designed by Giorgetti and Magrini, launched in 1986. Like *New Zealand* and many other Twelves, she took part in the World Championships. A good performance was marred by the loss of crew on several occasions.

Length Overall	19.55 metres
Waterline length	13.60 metres
Sail Area	210 square metres
Hull	Aluminium
Launched	1986
Owner	Consorzio Italia
Designer	Giorgetti & Magrini
Builder	Baglietto Shipyard
Skipper	Aldo Migliaccio

Page 164: *French Kiss* French Challenge Candidate (1987)

The thinking behind the forceful *French Kiss* came from P. Briand, the notable French yacht designer. In the capable hands of Marc Pajot it raced well until beaten in the semi-final of the challengers' competition by *New Zealand*.

Length Overall	20.5 metres
Waterline length	13.5 metres
Hull	Aluminium
Launched	1986
Sponsor	S. Crasnianski/Kiss France
Designer	P. Briand
Builder	Alubat
Skipper	Marc Pajot

Page 165: *White Crusader* GB Challenge Candidate (1987)

Britain had considered entering a yacht designed by David Hollom for the 1987 America's Cup, but due to lack of development time Ian Howlett's *White Crusader* was chosen. Re-shaped and re-trimmed on several occasions, *White Crusader* showed great potential but did not perform as expected. Sometimes she beat stronger contenders, but more often than not she lost to yachts that were weaker, on paper at least.

Length Overall	19.9 metres
Draft	2.7 metres
Hull	Aluminium
Launched	1986
Owner	British America's Cup Challenges PLC
Builder	Cougar Marine
Skipper	H. Cudmore

Pages 166–167: *Azzura II* **Italian Challenge Candidate (1987)**

The second Vallicelli designed Twelve, *Azzura II*, was launched in 1986 and competed in the World Championships. She was not to fare well in the conditions either in the World Championships or in the America's Cup eliminators at Freemantle, and left the field earlier than expected.

Length Overall	20.05 metres
Waterline length	13.9 metres
Draft	2.85 metres
Hull	Aluminium
Launched	1986
Owner	Consorzio Azzura Sfida Italiana
Designer	A. Vallicelli
Builder	S.A.I. Ambrosini Shipyards
Skipper	M. Pelaschier

Page 168: *Stars & Stripes* **US Challenger (1987)**

It has been said that Dennis Conner did not sleep for the four years between 1983 and 1987. Even if this was because of his defeat with *Liberty*, the time gained allowed him to get it right with his fleet of *Stars & Stripes* yachts. Basing his campaign in Hawaii, where the waters matched those of Freemantle, Conner began with *Liberty* as a bench mark. He then experimented with *Stars & Stripes '83* (formerly *Spirit of America*, but re-worked by the Chance, Nelson and Pedrick design team). This led to *Stars & Stripes '85, '86* and finally *Stars & Stripes '87*. To win back some of the honour he had lost in 1983, he also turned to Grumman Aerospace for help, to ensure that his boat would be successful in the forthcoming challenge.

Stars & Stripes had to be a powerful yacht to race in the Indian Ocean. Unlike the waters off Newport,

those off Freemantle were high and each boat in the Louis Vuitton challenger's competition had a horror story to tell, such as men washed overboard into the shark-infested waters or, in the case of *White Crusader*, a broken mast.

Conner kept the potential of *Stars & Stripes* to himself and his team. Before the finals began, *New Zealand*, with her fibre-glass hull, was very much the favourite. But *Stars & Stripes* demolished the opposition. And she went on to demolish the defender. In the first race, Conner established a one minute and fifteen second lead at the first mark and then edged away to win by one minute and forty-one seconds. The second race, sailed in strong winds, also went to *Stars & Stripes*, as did the third. It seemed that only a disaster could prevent Dennis Conner from winning back the America's Cup. In one of the most perfect starts to an America's Cup race, Conner crossed the start line of the fourth race at the same time as the gun was fired, immediately creeping six seconds in front of *Kookaburra III*. He was not to lose the lead and ended up winning the race by one minute and sixteen seconds, and the series by four races to none. The Cup was once more America's.

Length Overall	67 feet 3 inches
Waterline length	46 feet 4 inches
Draft	9 feet 2 inches
Sail Area	1,808 square feet
Hull	Aluminium
Launched	1986
Owner	Sail America Foundation
Designer	B. Chance/B. Nelson/D. Pedrick
Builder	R. Derecktor
Built	Rhode Island, USA
Skipper	Dennis Conner

Page 169: *Kookaburra III* **Australian Defender (1987)**

While the rest of the world had thirteen Twelve Metre yachts competing against each other for the right to challenge for the America's Cup, the Australians had to find a defender from nine boats taken from four camps. Syd Fisher's campaign was led by *Steak 'N Kidney*, who had raced against *Australia I* for practice. But *Steak 'N Kidney* was not quite in the running. Nor was Graham Spurling's *South Australia*. Alan Bond, desperate to wage a successful defence after winning the America's Cup in 1983, built *Australia III*. The 1986 World Championships were won by *Australia III*, with *Australia II* in fourth place. In spite of this it was felt that a new yacht was needed for the America's Cup, and Bond commissioned *Australia IV*.

Kevin Parry's two early *Kookaburras* were engaged in their own private trials and did not race in the World Championships. Almost identical to each other, they succeeded in confusing everyone as to which was *Kookaburra I* and which was *Kookaburra II* by exchanging sails and crews daily.

In the selection trials *Kookaburra III* fought with *Australia IV* and won. Alan Bond, the winning owner in 1983, had fallen by the wayside.

In the cup series itself *Kookaburra III* could do nothing to prevent Dennis Conner from regaining the cup he had lost and taking it to its new home, San Diego.

Length Overall	66 feet
Waterline length	45 feet
Draft	8 feet 9 inches
Hull	Aluminium
Sail Area	1,750 square feet
Launched	1986
Owner	Taskforce '87
Designer	J. Swarbrick/I. Murray
Builder	Parry Boatbuilders
Built	Freemantle, Australia
Skipper	Iain Murray

Page 170: *New Zealand* **challenges** *Stars & Stripes* **(1988)**

It is disheartening that a yacht race of such standing should end up being fought in a courtroom and not at sea. It is true that controversy has been no stranger to America's Cup competition; there was Dunraven's protest in 1895 and *Australia II*'s winged hull led to American protests. The 1988 challenge, however, began in the courts and ended in the courts.

On 4 February 1987, Dennis Conner won back the America's Cup from Australia and returned home to San Diego. With no race announcement made by the Americans, Michael Fay issued a New Zealand challenge on 17 July. His monohull yacht, *New Zealand*, was twice the size of the standard Twelve Metre – one hundred and twenty three feet overall and ninety feet at the waterline. Fay also proposed that the challenge should be fought in June 1988, just eleven months away.

The Americans initially refused. Then in December, after a number of court rulings, San Diego grudgingly accepted New Zealand's challenge and one month later Conner announced his decision to defend the cup in a sixty-foot catamaran. In April 1988 Britain requested permission to join the challenge and was soon followed by Australia. The Americans agreed, but New Zealand did not. The challenge would be between America and New Zealand.

After yet more legal wrangles, racing commenced in September 1988. Dennis Conner in his superfast catamaran won the best of three series. New Zealand then protested: catamarans did not comply with the rules. The protest was upheld and Judge Carmen Ciparick awarded the cup to the challengers. However, in April 1990 the Appeal Court delivered its final verdict and San Diego was declared the rightful winner of the challenge.

(Photograph reproduced courtesy of the Rosenfeld Collection Mystic Seaport Museum.)

DIGEST OF MATCH RESULTS

Date	Name	Rating	Course Length	Time Allowance		Elapsed Time			Corrected Time			Wins by	
				mins	secs	hrs	mins	secs	hrs	mins	secs	mins	secs
22 Aug 1851	*America*	170 tons	58 miles	–	–	10	37	00				8	00
	Aurora	47 tons		–	–	10	45	00					
		Waterline area											
8 Aug 1870	*Magic*	1680.0	35.1 miles	14	7	4	07	54	3	58	21	39	17
	Cambria	2105.8		–	–	4	34	37	4	37	38		
		Displacement											
16 Oct 1871	*Columbia*	1691	35.1 miles	1	41	6	17	42	6	19	41	27	04
	Livonia	1881		–	–	6	43	00	6	46	45		
18 Oct 1871	*Columbia*	1591	49 miles	6	10½	3	01	33½	3	07	41¾	10	33¾
	Livonia	1881		–	–	3	06	49½	3	18	51½		
19 Oct 1871	*Livonia*	1881	35.1 miles	–	–	3	53	05	4	02	25	15	10
	Columbia	1691		4	23	4	12	38	4	17	35		
21 Oct 1871	*Sappho*	1957	40 miles	–	–	5	33	21	5	36	02	33	21
	Livonia	1881		2	07	6	04	38	6	09	23		
23 Oct 1871	*Sappho*	1957	40 miles	1	09	4	38	05	4	46	17	25	27
	Livonia	1881		–	–	5	04	41	5	11	44		
		Cubical contents											
11 Aug 1876	*Madeleine*	8199.17	32.6 miles	1	01	5	24	55	5	23	54	10	59
	Countess of Dufferin	9028.40		–	–	5	34	53	5	34	53		
12 Aug 1876	*Madeleine*	8199.17	40 miles	1	01	7	19	47	7	18	46	27	14
	Countess of Dufferin	9028.40		–	–	7	46	00	7	46	00		
9 Nov 1881	*Mischief*	3931.90	32.6 miles	–	–	4	17	09	4	17	06	28	20¼
	Atalanta	3567.60		2	55¼	4	48	24½	4	45	29¼		
10 Nov 1881	*Mischief*	3931.90	32 miles	–	–	4	54	53	4	54	53	38	54
	Atalanta	3567.60		2	55	5	36	52	5	33	47		
		Length and Sail Area											
14 Sept 1885	*Puritan*	83.85 (Sail Tons)	32.6 miles	–	–	6	06	05	6	06	05	16	19
	Genesta	83.05		0	28	6	22	52	6	22	24		
16 Sept 1885	*Puritan*	83.85	40 miles	–	–	5	03	14	5	03	14	1	38
	Genesta	83.05		0	28	5	05	20	5	04	52		
9 Sept 1886	*Mayflower*	87.99	32.6 miles	–	–	5	26	41	5	26	41	12	02
	Galatea	86.87		0	38	5	39	21	5	38	43		
11 Sept 1886	*Mayflower*	87.99	40 miles	–	–	6	49	00	6	49	00	29	09
	Galatea	86.87		0	38	7	18	48	7	18	09		
27 Sept 1887	*Volunteer*	89.10	32.6 miles	–	–	4	53	18	4	53	18	19	23¾
	Thistle	88.46		0	05¾	5	12	46	5	12	40¼		
30 Sept 1887	*Volunteer*	89.10	40 miles	–	–	5	42	56¼	5	42	56¾	11	48¾
	Thistle	88.46		0	06	5	54	51	5	54	45		
7 Oct 1893	*Vigilant*	96.78	30 miles	–	–	4	05	47	4	05	47	5	48
	Valkyrie II	93.11		1	48	4	13	23	4	11	35		
9 Oct 1893	*Vigilant*	96.78	30 miles	–	–	3	25	01	3	25	01	10	35
	Valkyrie II	93.11		1	48	3	37	24	3	35	36		
13 Oct 1893	*Vigilant*	96.78	30 miles	–	–	3	24	39	3	24	39	0	40
	Valkyrie II[1]	93.57		1	33	3	26	52	3	25	19		
7 Sept 1895	*Defender*	100.36	30 miles	0	29	5	00	24	4	59	55	8	49
	Valkyrie III	100.49		–	–	5	08	44	5	08	44		
10 Sept 1895	*Valkyrie III*	100.40	30 miles	–	–	3	55	09	3	55	09	0	47
	Defender	100.36		0	29	3	56	25	3	55	56		

Date	Name	Rating	Course Length	Time Allowance		Elapsed Time			Corrected Time			Wins by	
				mins	secs	hrs	mins	secs	hrs	mins	secs	mins	secs
12 Sept 1895	Defender	100.36	30 miles	0	29	4	44	12	4	43	43		
	Valkyrie III	100.49		–	–				Did not finish				
16 Oct 1899	Columbia	102.135	30 miles	–	–	4	53	53	4	53	53	10	08
	Shamrock I	101.092		0	06	5	04	07	5	04	01		
17 Oct 1899	Columbia	102.135	30 miles	–	–	3	37	00	3	37	00		
	Shamrock I	101.092		0	06				Did not finish				
20 Oct 1899	Columbia	102.135	30 miles	0	16	3	38	25	3	38	09	6	34
	Shamrock I[1]	102.565		–	–	3	44	43	3	44	43		
28 Sept 1901	Columbia	102.355	30 miles	0	43	4	31	07	4	30	24	1	20
	Shamrock II	103.79		–	–	4	31	44	4	31	44		
3 Oct 1901	Columbia	102.355	30 miles	0	43	3	13	18	3	12	35	3	35
	Shamrock II	103.79		–	–	3	16	10	3	16	10		
4 Oct 1901	Columbia	102.355	30 miles	0	43	4	33	40	4	32	57	0	41
	Shamrock II	103.79		–	–	4	33	38	4	33	38		
22 Aug 1903	Reliance	108.41	30 miles	–	–	3	32	17	3	32	17	7	03
	Shamrock III	104.37		1	57	3	41	17	3	39	20		
25 Aug 1901	Reliance	108.41	30 miles	–	–	3	14	54	3	14	54	1	19
	Shamrock III	104.37		1	57	3	18	10	3	16	12		
3 Sept 1901	Reliance	108.41	30 miles	–	–	4	28	00	4	28	00		
	Shamrock III	104.37		1	57				Did not finish				
		Sail Area Limits & Penalties											
15 July 1920	Shamrock IV	93.8 (Rating	30 miles	6	42	4	24	58	4	24	58		
	Resolute	83.5 length)		–	–				Did not finish				
20 July 1920	Shamrock IV	94.4	30 miles	7	01	5	33	18	5	22	18	2	26
	Resolute	83.5		–	–	5	31	45	5	24	44		
21 July 1920	Resolute	83.5	30 miles	–	–	4	03	06	3	56	05	7	01
	Shamrock IV	94.4		7	01	4	03	06	3	49	04		
23 July 1920	Resolute	83.5	30 miles	–	–	3	37	52	3	31	12	9	58
	Shamrock IV[1]	93.8		6	40	3	41	10	3	41	10		
27 July 1920	Resolute	83.5	30 miles	–	–	5	35	15	5	28	35	19	45
	Shamrock IV	93.8		6	40	5	48	20	5	48	20		

"J" CLASS

Date	Name	Course Length	Elapsed Time			Wins by	
			hrs	mins	secs	mins	secs
13 Sept 1930	Enterprise	30 miles	4	03	48	2	52
	Shamrock V		4	06	40		
15 Sept 1930	Enterprise	30 miles	4	00	44	9	34
	Shamrock V		4	10	18		
17 Sept 1930	Enterprise	30 miles	3	56	16	–	–
	Shamrock V		Did not finish				
18 Sept 1930	Enterprise	30 miles	3	10	13	5	44
	Shamrock V		3	15	57		
17 Sept 1934	Endeavour	30 miles	3	43	44	2	09
	Rainbow		3	45	53		
18 Sept 1934	Endeavour	30 miles	3	09	01	0	51
	Rainbow		3	09	52		
20 Sept 1934	Rainbow	30 miles	4	35	34	3	26
	Endeavour		4	39	00		
22 Sept 1934	Rainbow	30 miles	3	15	38	1	15
	Endeavour		3	16	53		
24 Sept 1934	Rainbow	30 miles	3	54	05	4	01
	Endeavour		3	58	06		

[1] Remeasured.

Date	Name	Course Length	Elapsed Time			Wins by	
			hrs	mins	secs	mins	secs
25 Sept 1934	*Rainbow*	30 miles	3	40	05	0	55
	Endeavour		3	41	00		
2 Aug 1937	*Ranger*	30 miles	4	41	15	17	05
	Endeavour II		4	58	20		
4 Aug 1937	*Ranger*	30 miles	3	54	30	4	27
	Endeavour II		3	58	57		
5 Aug 1937	*Ranger*	30 miles	3	07	49	3	37
	Endeavour II		3	11	26		

TWELVE METRE CLASS

Date	Name	Course Length	Elapsed Time			Wins by	
			hrs	mins	secs	mins	secs
20 Sept 1958	*Columbia*	24 miles	5	13	46	7	43
	Sceptre		5	21	29		
21 Sept 1958	*Columbia*	24 miles	Time limit				
	Sceptre		expired				
24 Sept 1958	*Columbia*	24 miles	3	17	40	11	40
	Sceptre		3	29	20		
25 Sept 1958	*Columbia*	24 miles	3	09	02	8	21
	Sceptre		3	17	23		
26 Sept 1958	*Columbia*	24 miles	3	04	12	6	52
	Sceptre		3	11	04		
15 Sept 1962	*Weatherly*	24 miles	3	13	45	3	32
	Gretel		3	17	17		
18 Sept 1962	*Gretel*	24 miles	2	46	47	1	41
	Weatherly		2	47	28		
20 Sept 1962	*Weatherly*	24 miles	4	20	52	8	43
	Gretel		4	29	35		
22 Sept 1962	*Weatherly*	24 miles	3	22	09	0	22
	Gretel		3	22	31		
25 Sept 1962	*Weatherly*	24 miles	3	16	04	3	44
	Gretel		3	19	48		
15 Sept 1964	*Constellation*	24 miles	3	30	41	5	34
	Sovereign		3	36	15		
17 Sept 1964	*Constellation*	24.3 miles	3	46	48	20	24
	Sovereign		4	07	12		
19 Sept 1964	*Constellation*	24.3 miles	3	38	07	6	33
	Sovereign		3	44	00		
21 Sept 1964	*Constellation*	24.3 miles	4	12	27	15	40
	Sovereign		4	28	07		
12 Sept 1967	*Intrepid*	24.3 miles	3	24	47	5	58
	Dame Pattie		3	30	45		
13 Sept 1967	*Intrepid*	24.3 miles	3	29	06	3	36
	Dame Pattie		3	32	42		
14 Sept 1967	*Intrepid*	24.3 miles	3	20	07	4	41
	Dame Pattie		3	24	48		
18 Sept 1967	*Intrepid*	24.3 miles	3	27	35	3	35
	Dame Pattie		3	31	10		
15 Sept 1970	*Intrepid*	24.3 miles	3	25	57	5	52
	Gretel II		3	31	49		
20 Sept 1970	*Gretel II*	24.3 miles	Start time			1	07
	Intrepid		not recorded				

Date	Name	Course Length	Elapsed Time			Wins by	
			hrs	mins	secs	mins	secs
22 Sept 1970	*Intrepid*	24.3 miles	3	24	34	1	18
	Gretel II		3	25	52		
24 Sept 1970	*Gretel II*	24.3 miles	3	33	38	1	02
	Intrepid		3	34	40		
26 Sept 1970	*Intrepid*	24.3 miles	4	28	52	1	44
	Gretel II		4	29	36		
10 Sept 1974	*Courageous*	24.3 miles	4	11	57	4	54
	Southern Cross		4	16	51		
12 Sept 1974	*Courageous*	24.3 miles	3	32	28	1	11
	Southern Cross		3	33	39		
16 Sept 1974	*Intrepid*	24.3 miles	3	32	01	5	27
	Southern Cross		3	37	28		
17 Sept 1974	*Courageous*	24.3 miles	3	32	18	7	19
	Southern Cross		3	39	37		
13 Sept 1977	*Courageous*	24.3 miles	Finish time			1	48
	Australia		not recorded				
15 Sept 1977	*Courageous*	24.3 miles	Time limit				
	Australia		expired				
16 Sept 1977	*Courageous*	24.3 miles	3	44	05	1	03
	Australia		3	45	08		
17 Sept 1977	*Courageous*	24.3 miles	4	23	08	2	22
	Australia		4	25	30		
18 Sept 1977	*Courageous*	24.3 miles	3	32	22	2	25
	Australia		3	34	47		
16 Sept 1980	*Freedom*	24. 3 miles	3	48	03	1	52
	Australia		3	49	55		
19 Sept 1980	*Australia*	24.3 miles	5	06	28	0	28
	Freedom		5	06	56		
21 Sept 1980	*Freedom*	24.3 miles	3	35	05	0	53
	Australia		3	35	58		
23 Sept 1980	*Freedom*	24.3 miles	3	41	12	3	48
	Australia		3	45	00		
24 Sept 1980	*Freedom*	24.3 miles	3	07	52	3	38
	Australia		3	11	30		
13 Sept 1983	*Liberty*	24.4 miles	3	25	50	1	10
	Australia II		3	27	00		
15 Sept 1983	*Liberty*	24.4 miles	3	49	14	0	33
	Australia II		3	49	47		
17 Sept 1983·	*Australia II*	24.4 miles	Time limit				
	Liberty		expired				
18 Sept 1983	*Australia II*	24.4 miles	3	50	24	3	14
	Liberty		3	53	46		
20 Sept 1983	*Liberty*	24.4 miles	3	29	11	0	43
	Australia II		3	29	54		
21 Sept 1983	*Australia II*	24.4 miles	3	29	56	1	47
	Liberty		3	31	43		
22 Sept 1983	*Australia II*	24.4 miles	3	31	36	3	25
	Liberty		3	35	01		
26 Sept 1983	*Australia II*	24.4 miles	4	15	45	0	41
	Liberty		4	16	26		
31 Jan 1987	*Stars & Stripes*	24 miles	3	28	45	1	41
	Kookaburra III		3	30	26		
1 Feb 1987	*Stars & Stripes*	24 miles	3	02	19	1	13
	Kookaburra III		3	03	32		
2 Feb 1987	*Stars & Stripes*	24 miles	3	09	56	1	46
	Kookaburra III		3	11	42		
4 Feb 1987	*Stars & Stripes*	24 miles	3	05	55	1	59
	Kookaburra III		3	03	56		

BIBLIOGRAPHY

Agnew, F. H. *History of the America's Cup, 1881 to 1899* (Glasgow, 1899)

Bavier, Bob *America's Cup Fever: An Inside View of Fifty Years of America's Cup Competition* (Lymington, 1980)

Bertrand, John *Born to Win: A Lifelong Struggle to Capture the America's Cup* (London, 1985)

Burnell, P. *Races for the America's Cup* (London, 1965)

Carrick, J. *The Pictorial History of the America's Cup Races* (London, 1965)

Chevalier, François and Taglang, Jacques *America's Cup Yacht Designs 1851–1986* (Paris, 1988)

Coffin, R. F. *The America's Cup: How It Was Won* (New York, 1885)

Conner, Dennis *Comeback: My Race for the America's Cup* (London, 1987)

Dear, Ian *The America's Cup: An Illustrated History* (London, 1983)

Dilke, Sir F. W. *Observer on Ranger during the Races for the America's Cup, 1937* (London, 1938)

Fisher, Bob *12-Metre Images* (London, 1986)

Fairchild, Tony *The America's Cup Challenge: There Is No Second* (London, 1983)

Grandison, H. J. *The America's Cup: Its Origin and History* (London, 1914)

Geilles, Daniel *La Cope de L'America* (Paris, 1977)

Hickley, D. *The Life and Times of the Late Sir Thomas J. Lipton from Cradle to Grave* (New York, 1932)

Illingworth, K. *Twenty Challenges for the America's Cup* (London, 1968)

Irving, J. *The King's Britannia: The Story of a Great Ship* (London, 1937)

John, Anthony *The Early Challenges for the America's Cup 1851–1937* (London, 1986)

Kemp, P. K. *Racing for the America's Cup* (London, 1937)

Mitchell, Carleton *Summer of the Twelves* (New York, 1959)

Morris, Everett *Sailing for the America's Cup* (New York, 1964)

New York Yacht Club *Report of the America's Cup Committee on the Match Defender against Valkyrie 1894–95* (New York, 1895)

New York Yacht Club *Report of the Committee of the New York Yacht Club Relating to Certain Changes Made by the Earl of Dunraven* (New York, 1896)

Rayner, Ranulf *The Paintings of the America's Cup, 1851–1987* (Newton Abbot, 1988)

Riggs, Doug *Keelhauled: Unsportsmanlike Conduct and the America's Cup* (London, 1986)

Rousmaniere, John *The America's Cup, 1851–1983* (London, 1983)

Sefton, Alan *The Inside Story of KZ-7: New Zealand's First America's Cup Challenge* (London, 1987)

Shafters, L. A. *The Cup Races: A History in Pictures* (New York, 1901)

Somerville, Hugh *Sceptre: The Seventeenth Challenger for the America's Cup* (London, 1958)

Southern, Leonard *Five Shamrocks and the America's Cup* (London, 1938)

Stone, H. L. *The America's Cup Races* (New York, 1930)

Stone, H. L. *Millions for Defence: A Pictorial History of the Races for the America's Cup* (New York, 1934)

Stone, Herbert and Taylor, William *The America's Cup Races* (Princeton, 1958)

Thompson, W. M. and Lawson, T. W. *History of the America's Cup* (Boston, 1902)

Vanderbilt, H. S. *Enterprise: The Story of the Defence of the America's Cup in 1930* (New York, 1931)

Vanderbilt, H. S. *On the Wind's Highway: Ranger, Rainbow and Racing* (New York, 1939)

Wheatley, Keith *America's Cup '87: The Inside Story* (London, 1986)